Minor Writings

On

Astrological Magic

Volume II

By Clifford Hartleigh Low

Edited by R. Weisserman

Copyright 2024 by Clifford Hartleigh Low

All rights reserved. No part of this publication may be reproduced, stored in a retrieval system, or transmitted, in any form or by any means, electronic, mechanical, photocopying, recording, or otherwise, without the prior written permission of the publisher.

Published in the United States by
Astrological Magic LLC,
830 E. Lawn Dr Teaneck,
NJ 07666 USA
E-mail: publishing@astrologicalmagic.com
Visit: www.astrologicalmagic.com

ISBN: 979-8-9893135-1-8

Table of Contents

Preface vii

Chapter One: Jupiter Talismans 1
    The Secret Powers of Jupiter 1
    The Ring of Success 4
    The Ring of Ultimate Fortune 7
    The Ring of Abundance 9
    Ring of Supreme Abundance 11
    Good Fortune and Many Sons 13

Chapter Two: Mars Talismans 15
    Powerful Petition to Mars 15
    Two Petitions to Mars 23

Chapter Three: Sun Talismans 28
    The Ring of Triumphing Light 29
    The Great Ring of Wealth: Marxois 33
    J.R.R. Tolkien's One Ring to Rule Them All 37
    First Sun in Aries Talismanic Election 44
    Second Sun in Aries Talismanic Election 46

Chapter Four: Venus Talismans 49
    A Venus Petition 50
    Magic Rings of Seduction 53
    The Ring of Dragonfire's Kiss 61
    The Ring of the Kiss of Darkness 65

Chapter Five: Mercury Talismans 75
    The Ring of the Green Lion 75

Talismans of Trust 77

Chapter Six: Moon Talismans 81

    Some Notes on the Operation of the Moon 81

    The Ring of the Serpent of Healing 85

    Talisman of Safe Driving 87

    The Talismans of the Inescapable Prison 92

    The Rings of Memory 96

    The Rings of the Fortunate Mystic 100

    The Talismans of Awestruck Dread 103

    Defixios of Burning Hatred 106

    The Rings of Fortunate Meetings 107

    The Talismans of Friendship and Love 110

    Talisman of Desire: Alahue 113

    The Gems of Bedazzling Ardor 117

    The Talismans of Union 120

Chapter Seven: Other Stellar Talismans 124

    Aries Medical Talismans 125

    Magic Rings of Procyon 133

    The Home Defense Rings of Al Tarf 153

    The Ring of the Casino 155

    The Ring of Fever's Eclipse 157

    The Ring of Splendor 160

    The Talismans of Turmantis 163

    The Rings of the Diplomat 169

    The Talismans of the Angel with the Backwards Head 174

Preface

The following records the creation of a series of talismans made in the tradition of Scholastic Image Magic, known to some as the Science of Images. This volume is intended to be a companion book with Volume I, which explains some of the context, history, and materials needed to begin practicing this craft.

Chapter One

Jupiter Talismans

The Secret Powers of Jupiter

The key to understanding Jupiter in a traditional context is that it is the most temperate of planets. It fills in whatever is lacking in every situation, and so it can be defined best by negatives. It is the absence of strife and poverty, the absence of ignorance and disorder, the negation of sorrow and weakness.

Things embodying Jupiter are often subtle because they are gentle; they are like the Air- the element most aligned with the planet. It is invisible except through indirect influences, and easily taken for granted unless during a gale or in a vacuum.

Under even minimally favorable circumstances, Jupiter keeps things going just fine and dandy, and everyone mistakenly thinks this is simple normalcy.

It is the Greater Benefic at its most magnanimous.

Contrary to what you may have heard, Jupiter talismans are fantastic for weight loss. Remember that Jupiter creates beauty moreso than Venus, and that Jupiter is a temperate planet and balances out all excesses and extremes. Even contemporary science reveals that symmetrical faces and bodies are deemed beautiful over unbalanced ones. Jupiter also governs exercise, and eases pain generally.

Jupiter's temperateness is a concept hard to convey in contemporary terms. Jupiter has the capacity to augment, but ultimately it is the active promotion of positive normalcy.

When you restore your device to default settings because it wasn't working correctly, you are engaged in something akin to the purpose of Jupiter. Long before the revisionists (for religious reasons) switched the colors of Jupiter, astrologers assigned to him the colors white and yellow. Today, I'd add khaki and taupe; the colors of mildness and normalcy. The colors of the neutral, reliable default settings.

Jupiter's powers are not those of inertia but the strength of the middle path. The Greater Benefic manifests through ordinary goodness in things.

Jupiter is used most prominently in healing magic and protective magic, because in both cases the ideal is physical normalcy and security from the difficult and abnormal.

This is why Jupiter is so hard to understand. It is the planet most defined in negatives; it is the planet most akin to the Air Element. It is invisible until something is awry. Unless one is suffocating in a vacuum or being blown about in a gale, one can easily forget that the atmosphere is not simply empty space. It is *not* empty space; it is what enables all life to be possible.

This is why Kabbalists felt that the intelligences of Jupiter were secret interlocutors to the godhead. It is the Divine which sets the defaults, which defines the rules, which establishes health and longevity and the good.

The cleanliness of the empty canvas or the unwritten page are not voids. They are abundances of possibilities. This is the secret of Jupiter- the hidden hand that always is helping, and often helping better because of its obscurity.

The abnormal is marvelous, but seldom is it entirely beneficial. The normal is taken for granted easily, but it is the doorway to the greater good. And this is the case because—in astrological terms at least—the Divine world has rigged cosmic law slightly in our favors. The default is, surprisingly, benevolent.

The Ring of Success

Jupiter Exalted, *Picatrix* Variant

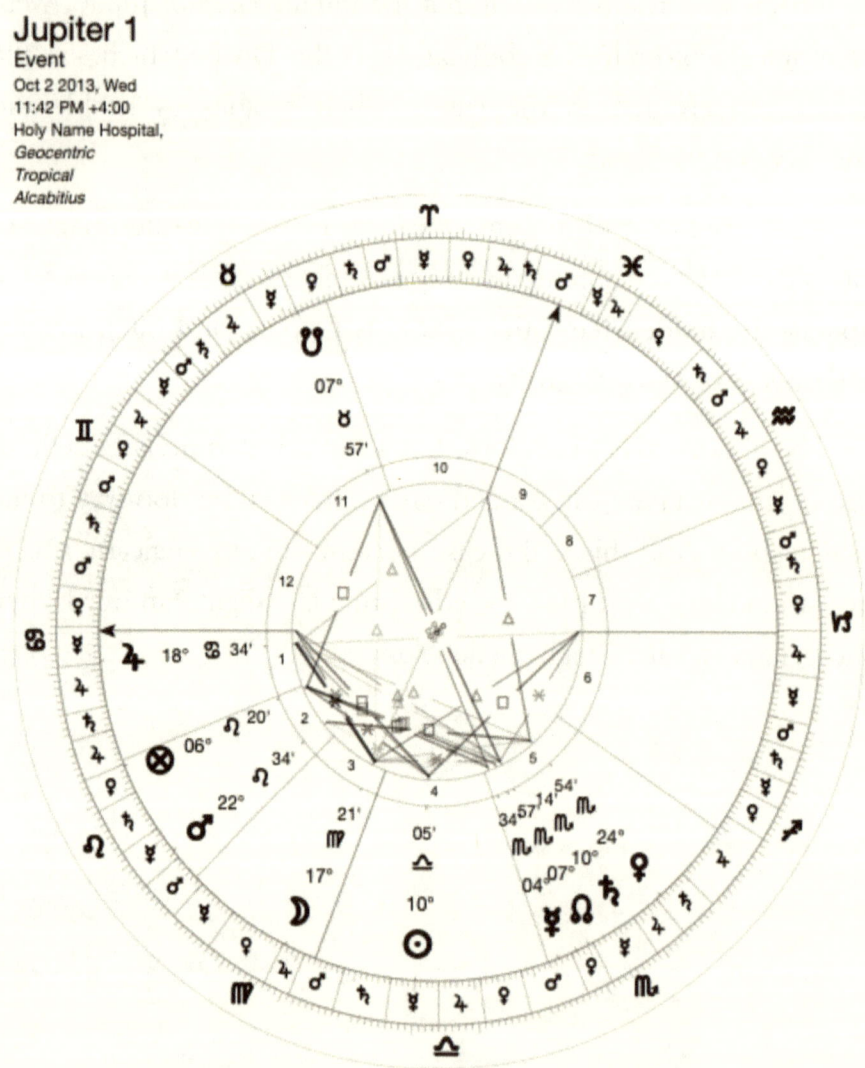

Picatrix II:10 *Rubeus* p.105: "The Image of Jupiter. Under the influence of Jupiter, make the figure of a crowned man sitting on a throne with four feet carried by four winged men and the man who is sitting on the throne is raising his hands as though he were praying.

Make it in the hour of Jupiter when Jupiter is rising in his exaltation and make it in a clear and white stone. Those who carry this image will have increase of riches and honor and lead a good life, and have many sons, and be able to perform good things and not be injured by enemies."

This was a talisman I was particularly looking forward to. It's as general a luck talisman as it gets–riches, safety, fame, freedom, nobility, and posterity in one single ring–which to me is useful because I only have ten fingers! I don't need many (or any) sons, but the rest sounds like a plan.

This was a very good election. Jupiter rose in his Hour, exalted. The Moon was sufficiently fast and aspected both benefics by sextile, and the aspect to Jupiter was very tight. The Moon was cadent but in in her Joy, so I don't think this was an issue. The Sun applied to square Jupiter but it was just barely out of orb and not a sufficient concern to nullify the election.

Everything else in this project was tough. Finding a white stone proved difficult. I wanted marble but none was available at short notice. I ended up using white agate where the striations were almost invisible.

Engraving such a complicated image on even large stones within the time period was challenging; ultimately the four angels were stick figures with wings that looked more like kidneys than something aerodynamic. But the enthroned king had the sigil of Jupiter over his heart, and his arms were spread wide (based on divination) rather than clasped in Christian prayer posture. I think the artistic effects are tertiary to all other factors, and the hierarchy of Jupiter surely recognize what the ring's design represents. I wish I could have done better, but time was short.

The metal was mainly gold-filled wire for strength, but with true gold wire wrapped around the band in order to increase the association of the rings with wealth. The suffumigation and herb was gum mastic this time, and the oil was Aunt Sally's Lucky Dream Oil. The petition was abbreviated from the *Picatrix* Jupiter petition texts. Four rings were made.

The Ring of Ultimate Fortune

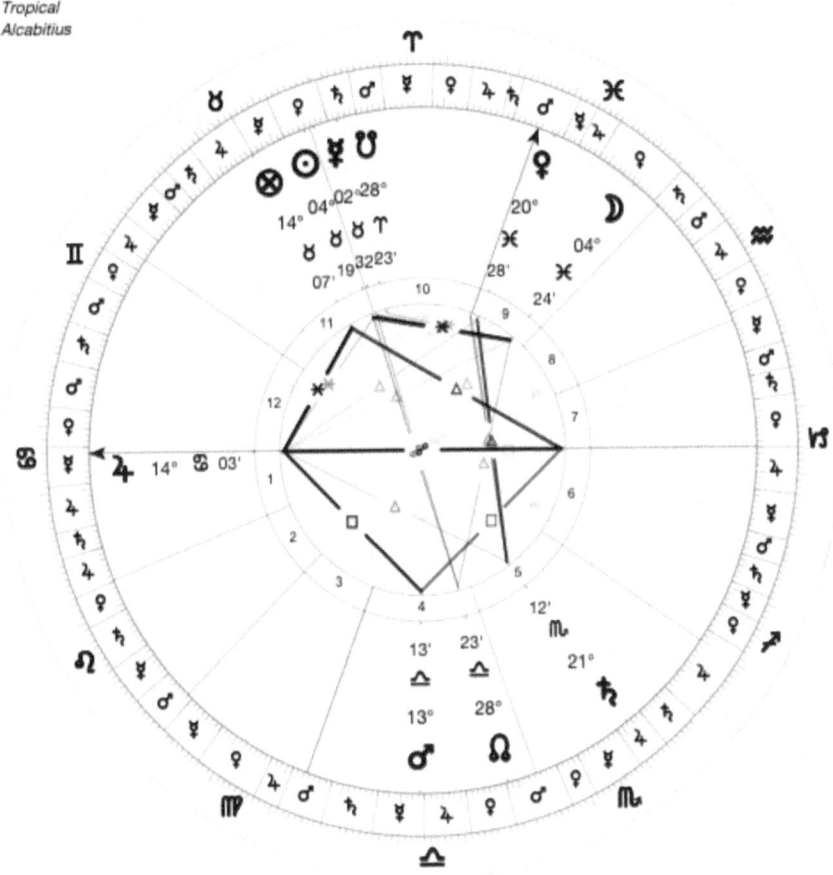

Jupiter was in his degree-of-exaltation, in his Day, with the Moon applying a lovely trine to him. The MC was furthermore fortified by Venus in her exaltation. The Moon was very fast, and the Dragon's Head was on the cusp of the 5th House–very fortunate indeed.

"The form of a man with the face of a lion and feet of a bird, and under his feet is a seven headed dragon and in his right hand he has a dart as though he wished to throw it at one of the dragon's heads."

As the election window was basically an hour long, I was able to use the longest of the *Picatrix* petition texts for Jupiter, beginning "May God bless you, Jupiter, planet of perfect and noble nature, exalted, honored, precious, and benign lord, warm and moist and similar in your nature to air, equitable in your works, wise, truthful, lover of religion..."

Text subsequent to this image in *Picatrix* but seemingly for a different election may well apply here too: "Whoever caries this ring will be served by the sons of men, eagles, vultures, lions, and all the works of Jupiter."

Three emerald rings were engraved thusly, set in a band of gold and gold-filled wire. The emerald was made affordable by having my jeweler make cabochons from rock. The emerald is highly included, and looks a fair bit like pale malachite; quite beautiful. Adam & Eve Oil was used, and the suffumigation was pine resin and rosebuds. The herb beneath the rings was violet leaf.

In addition, I engraved sigils of Jupiter (the Arabic *Picatrix* versions) on a pair of carnelian cufflinks and a tie tack, and two mineral orbs; one of quartz and the other of labradorite.

Overall, a project that I'm very proud of and satisfied by. We won't see anything like this again for a very long time.

(The election nearly got botched by disclosing it to someone in advance, but I was able to make some changes to the operation which saved it from nullification. Gotta be more careful about that.)

Smaller emerald cabochons have been put aside for Mercury talismans, someday.

The Ring of Abundance

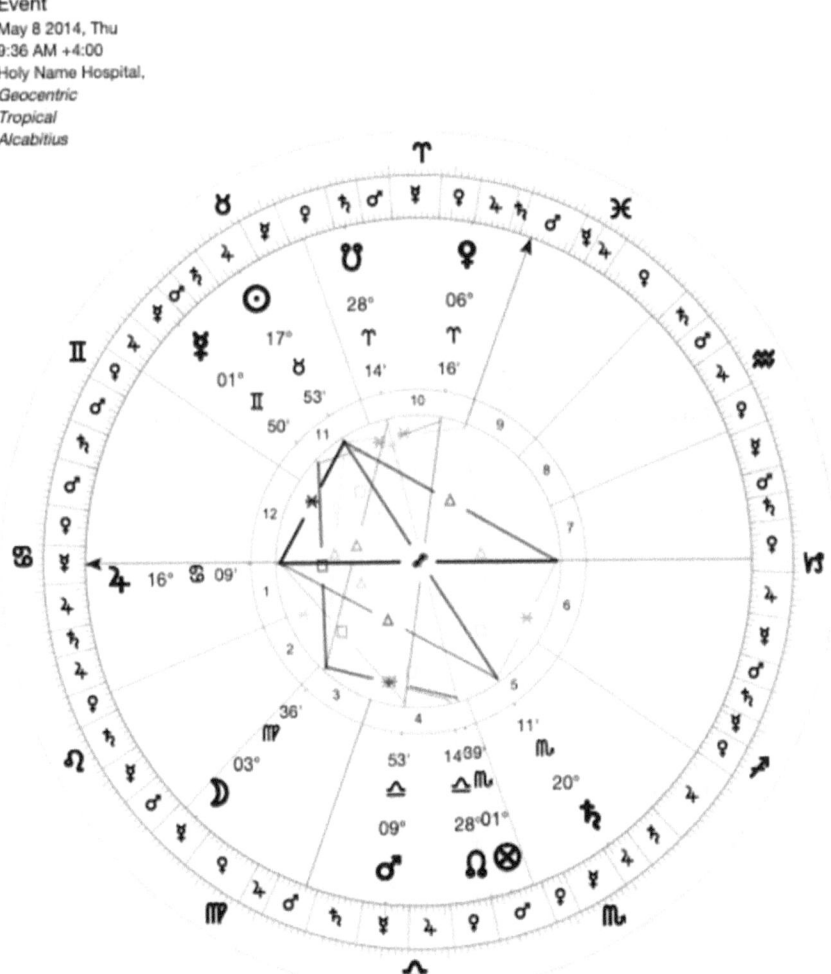

Jupiter ascended on Jupiter day. The Moon was making applying benevolent aspects to both Jupiter and the Pars Fortuna, strengthening it notably. The Moon itself was fairly slow but this was rectified by having a benefic on the ASC. The main downside was that Jupiter was making a trine to a retrograde Saturn; some may not even consider this an affliction, but I tend to think that Jupiter and Saturn have natural affinities for each other and this at worst is a lesser affliction.

The rings were carnelian, the bands gold-filled wire and gold wire wrap. The suffumigation was a blend of violet leaves, lignum aloes, and gum mastic. The herb beneath the stone was liquid storax. The long petition from *Picatrix* was used again, and the larger rings utilized the lion-headed dragon-stomping warrior and the smaller used the conventional symbol of Jupiter and the planet's name. No oil was used this time.

But the most interesting aspect of this election was that it was not performed alone. It was a training session for my new assistant and old friend, Kat Lunoe. She performed her tasks admirably, and in fact recited her petition far better than I, and her artistic skills were noticeable assets in the inscriptions of her images and sigils. (She also corrected me when I accidentally got the petition text pages out of order, for which I am especially grateful.)

Together we prepared nine rings. I was greatly surprised that by the time we had affixed the storax, Jupiter was exactly on the Ascendant; suggesting that we could easily have prepared nine *more* rings at least had I been wise enough to purchase more rings for the project. If we had restricted ourselves to sigils alone, we could easily have prepared forty rings during the same time frame.

The objective now is to produce large numbers of talismanic rings (and talismans of other varieties) during particularly excellent elections, rare elections, or of talismans which are especially sought-after. For sale someday, gifts for friends, and so on.

Ring of Supreme Abundance
Jupiter in Degree of Exaltation

Twelve large and small beryl cabochons were set in gold-filled/rolled-gold wire rings. Liquid storax mixed with glue was set beneath the rings, and the suffumigation was storax mixed with dried basil.

The Day is of Jupiter according to Christian and Chaldaean sources, though not Hour. The Moon is sufficiently fast, in Triplicity, just barely in Joy, Angular, and applying to conjoin Mercury in strong Essential Dignity by multiple qualities. According to some sources, the Moon just escaping combustion is an affliction and others deem it a fortitude- I take the latter view and this is the case here- rather tightly in fact.

The Moon is separating from an aspect with Jupiter though arguably out of orb. Normally I'd consider this a problem, but Jupiter DoE doesn't come terribly often and this is otherwise a pretty decent election. Jupiter is conjoining the Part of Fortune, which most likely repairs the separating aspect if it were an issue at all.

In any case, Moon afflictions are rectified with a Benefic on the ASC or MC and that makes Jupiter and Venus talisman elections a heck of a lot easier than the others.

The ASC is dominated by Jupiter and the MC is Ruled by Jupiter.

I also made a Jupiter DoE tie tack in white chalcedony with storax beneath; I can't get assurances most chalcedonies are untreated, undyed, and natural so this was a mild risk.

Attire was all white; rather than choosing religious garb, I wore items stereotypically associated with American upper classes–with the exception of the two white baseball caps emblazoned with countless dollar signs I alternated between during the long incantation from *Picatrix*.

The Sigil was from the Latin *Picatrix* over the word "JUPITER" in English. The oil was Jupiter Oil from Luckymojo.com.

Good Fortune and Many Sons
Loose White Stone Jupiter Talismans

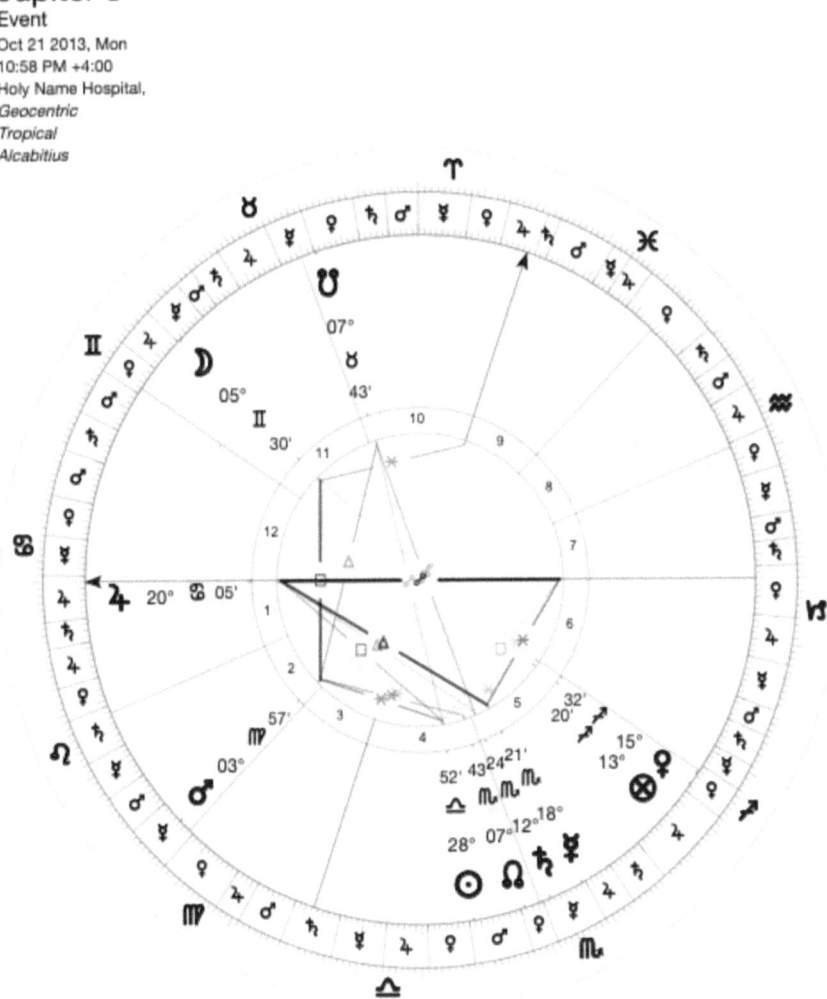

Jupiter is unafflicted and Rising in his Hour. The Moon is applying to Venus, though the aspect is adverse. *Picatrix* would deem this a mild fortitude. The Moon's Sign Ruler is not cadent, though SR- not a significant consideration from what I recall. The Lunar

Mansion is of a benevolent nature though the Moon is somewhat slow. The Moon is applying to conjoin Jupiter's antiscion; probably doesn't hurt. Jupiter is closely applying to the fixed star Castor, which may make it more durable in effects.

The stone was white dolomite. The suffumigation was storax. The oil was Luckymojo Jupiter Oil. No herb was used; these gems are intended to be carried in a mojo-style bag loosely filled with Jovian herbs in one's pocket. Six were made.

"Under the influence of Jupiter, make the figure of a crowned man sitting on a throne with four feet carried by four winged men and the man who is sitting on the throne is raising his hands as though he were praying. Make it in the hour of Jupiter when Jupiter is rising in his exaltation and make it in a clear and white stone. Those who carry this image will have increase of riches and honor and lead a good life, and have many sons, and be able to perform good things and not be injured by enemies."

Chapter Two

Mars Talismans

Powerful Petition to Mars

Ascendant ruler applying to trine Mars, with elaborate garb and suffumigations

Mars 1
Event
Jan 21 2018, Sun
3:32 PM +4:00
Holy Name Hospital,
Geocentric
Tropical
Alcabitius

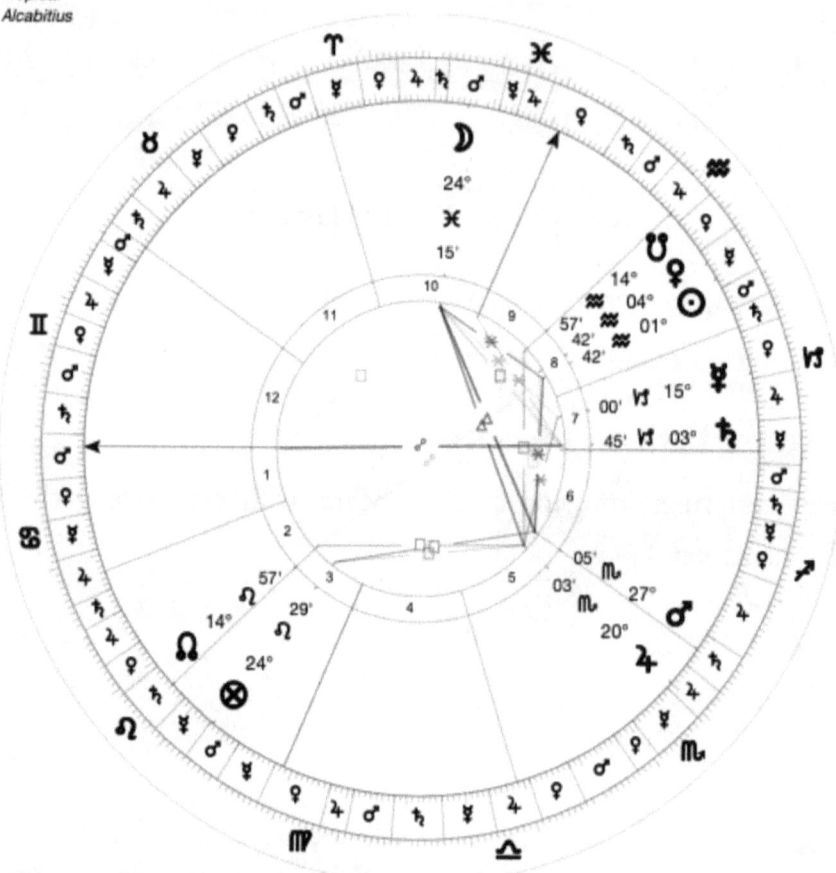

    A significant part of the tradition that Scholastic Image Magic is based upon includes celestial petitions. These are not technically image magic, because talismans are usually not involved. Nor are they properly scholastic, because they go beyond the boundaries of natural magic and invoke spirits directly, albeit ones who govern aspects of the natural world. They are prominently featured in *Picatrix,* but belong to the tradition of theurgy going back to at least

Iamblichus. The more unsavory variations of it can sometimes be classified as necromancy, by the medieval definitions of the term.

Nobody agrees what the nature of the spirits invoked are; some believe them to be angels, others djinn, others demons. Those informed by gnostic thought sometimes believe them to be archons. All agree that they are one of the principal origins of the legends of wish-granting spirits, such as in the story of Aladdin and the djinn. I believe them to be angels, in the sense that they are honorable servants of cosmic order; they are not always benevolent in action, but absolutely serve the greater good.

The celestial petition is a supplicatory appeal for aid in a sphere that the hierarchy in question has authority over. The timing is elected, the petitional text is very formal in structure, the suffumigations are very complex, ritual postures are used, and ritualized garb or costume is required. Sacrifices were also traditionally made, though this is seldom practical today. Planetary dieting is of great benefit to petitions, in addition to regimens of meditation and abstinence preceding the ceremony.

Though the type of elections used in celestial petitions differ from those used in the creation of talismans, they have enough similarity that formalized petitional texts are often used in the process of talismanic creation (abbreviated versions may be used if the electional window is brief).

Making talismans is hard work, from the election to their initial usage. Petitions are harder. Active preparation for a petition can sometimes be longer than a week. That is why when I do petitions for clients I usually charge more. To my knowledge I am the only magician commercially offering celestial petitions in the manner described in *Picatrix*.

Asking a talisman for a wish is effective and can be done many times, but their function is usually passive. Asking powerful governors of large portions of the cosmos for a boon is more effective—if the ritual is performed correctly—and what is asked for is granted in a very active way. An imperfect talisman may work, sometimes with side effects. If sufficiently flawed, they may do nothing, or could even curse the user. However, an imperfect petition may insult the hierarchy and cause the magician's prompt death. Petitions are high risk, and less forgiving of error.

For me, that makes it all the more exciting.

To elect a planetary petition, the planet of the hierarchy one is petitioning must be dignified and unafflicted in a way similar familiar to those who make planetary talismans, with some additional requirements and preferences as specified in *Picatrix*. The planet ruling the Ascendant must make a benevolent applying aspect to the petitioned planet. When possible, the Moon should also be dignified, unafflicted and forming a meaningful connection between the planet of the Ascendant and that of the petitioned planet. Ideally, none of the relevant planetary bodies will be cadent.

In the above election, the ruler of the Ascendant is the Moon, which simplifies a lot. The Ascendant and Moon are significators of the petitioner, and when they are in agreement the working is stronger; when they are the same body there are fewer factors to weigh.

The Moon is slow, but not prohibitively. When the Moon is slow but above twelve degrees of diurnal motion it is ideal for curses and malevolence, and so it is in harmony with at least part of the petition- it is of a destructive or disruptive nature. The Moon has some dignity within Pisces, being of the watery triplicity. The Moon exactly culminates while making a very tight applying trine with Mars. Mars is in domicile towards the end of Scorpio; he is not in the final two degrees of the Sign which could have been a problem. Mars is succedent in the 5th House. Mars is unfortunate in this House, but the other factors supersede this. Saturn is safely past opposition to the Ascendant, but is in the 6th House. The ruler of the Moon's Sign is itself the Moon, so it cannot be cadent; the beginning will be fulfilled and the end will be fulfilled. The Ascendant ruler is less essentially dignified than the Descendant ruler, but much more accidentally dignified. The largest shortcoming of the election is that Mars neither has the Hour or Day of the election; but *Picatrix* does not require this.

This is not a perfect election for a petition, but a solidly good one.

"When you wish to ask Mars for something, and speak to him and honor him, put him in a good condition as we have said... Dress yourself in red garments, and put a red linen or silk cloth on your head as well as a red skullcap, and hang a sword from your neck, and arm yourself with all the weapons you can carry; and dress yourself in the manner of a soldier or a fighter, and put a bronze ring on your finger. Take a bronze thurible with burning charcoal, in which you should put the following suffumigation." *-Picatrix*

One of my clients asked for a boon which was of a Martial nature, and so I sought a petitional election. After months of searching, this is the best one I found, and so I got to work.

I already had a cylindrical red chef cap for ritual purposes. It was neither a skullcap nor linen nor silk, but fulfilled the conditions acceptably.

My thurible was iron, which is a suitable substitute as the metal of Mars.

I could not figure out how to hang my sword comfortably from my neck; it's pretty heavy. Instead I found a pendant online in the shape of a winged sword, in steel—especially appropriate for Mars.

Similarly, I found a bronze ring in the shape of a crow's skull. Crows are birds of Mars according to both Lilly and Agrippa.

I purchased military-style camouflage print pants in red, and wore a rather spectacular polyester shirt with a flame print.

Finally, I slung a black bowie knife and sheath on a cord about my neck, tucked my hunting rifle under one arm, and held my Smith & Wesson revolver in my right hand. Both were loaded.

I probably looked completely terrifying, which is exactly what you should go for when petitioning the cruel lord of violence and dread.

"Take wormwood, aloes, squill, spurge, long pepper, and watercress in equal amounts. Grind them up and mix them with human blood. Make pills of this, which you may set aside for use. When you wish to begin working, put one of them into the thurible, which you have brought with you to a remote place specially set aside for this working. When you have arrived there, stand upright on your feet and speak secretly, boldly, and without any fear, facing the south... As the smoke rises, say the following." *-Picatrix*

I obtained all of the ingredients, but somehow misplaced the long pepper. Rather than make pills, I mixed the wormwood, aloe, squill, spurge and watercress in a cup and drizzled human blood over them.

At the appointed time, I stood facing south and somberly and loudly intoned the petitional text, rising in volume to a crescendo.

O Mars, you who are an honored lord and are hot and dry, mighty, weighty, firm of heart, spiller of blood and giver of illnesses thereto! You are strong, hardy, acute, daring, shining, agile, and the lord of battles, pains, miseries, wounds, prisons, sorrows, and mixed and separated things, who has no fear or contemplation of anything, sole helper in all your effects and in investigations thereof, strong in calculation and will to conquer and to seek after fortune, cause of lawsuits and battles, doer of evil to the weak and the strong, lover of the sons of battle, vindicator of wicked people and those who do evil in the world. I ask of you and conjure you by your names and your qualities that exist in heaven, and by your slayings, and also by your petitions to the Lord God who placed power and strength in you, gathering them in you and separating them from other planets that you might have strength and power, victory over all and great vigor... *-Picatrix*

I can't tell you what the boon was for the client; it's confidential, and knowledge of the specifics may interfere with their outcomes.

I will say that Mars provides boons in many areas other than violence and misfortune; and while his hierarchy is Malefic, they often do great good. Challenging injustice, obliteration of disease, removing obstacles to love and sex, surgery, alchemy, and vanquishing pestilence are all within the sphere of Mars' influence.

Mars is a mighty ally and a terrible foe.

Forget neither.

Two Petitions to Mars

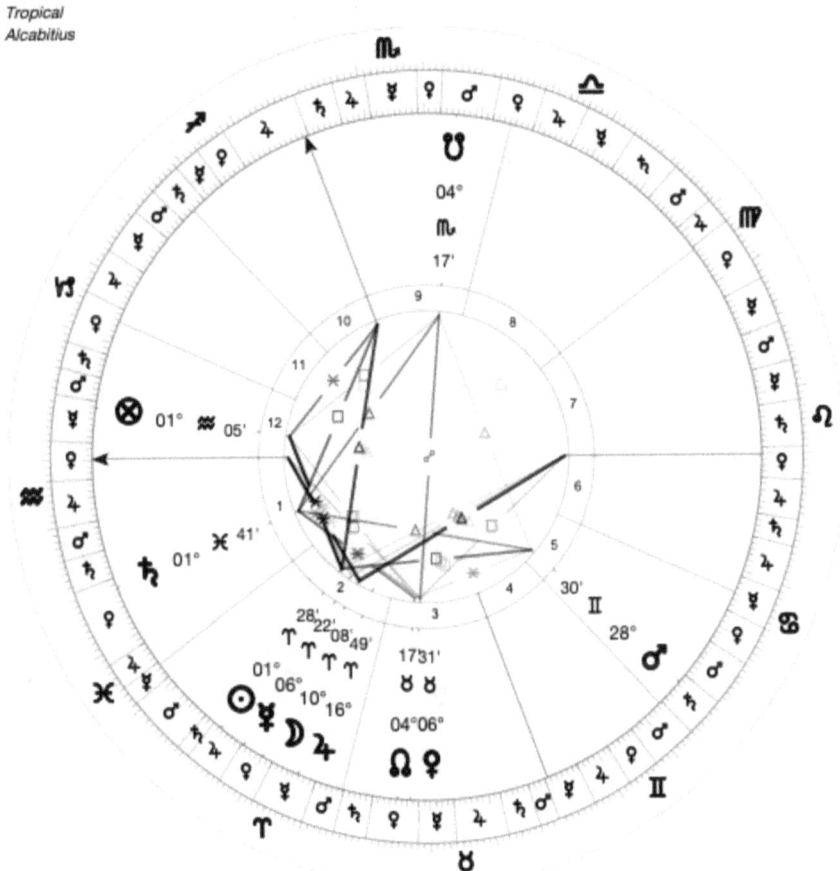

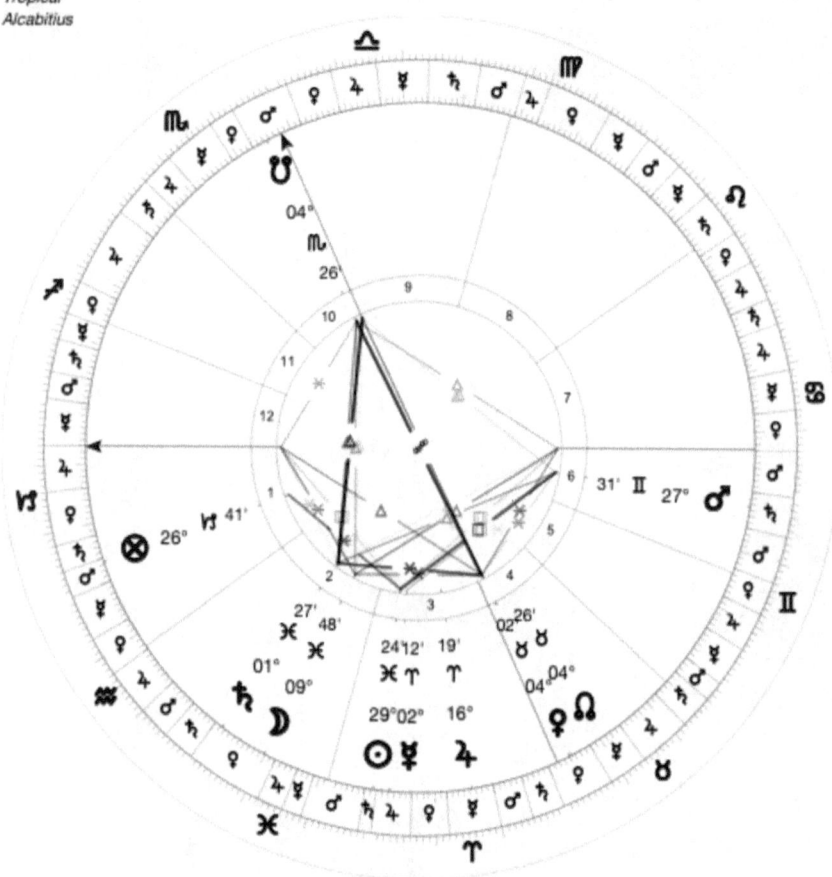

I did a pair of Mars petitions over a couple of days here. Both took advantage of the trine between Saturn and Mars, allowing Saturn to be the L1. In the first case I had Capricorn Rising and in the second Aquarius. The Moon was quite fast in both cases.

The Moon was unaspected in the first election, but applying to conjoin Jupiter loosely in the second. In the second election, the Moon had just escaped combustion- which I deem to be a strong accidental fortitude, though this view is in the minority. It certainly would be under-the-beams. Saturn was in Face currently; not a very nice Face but it does attain some meaningful dignity. Mars was in Term, which I tend to think is underestimated overall.

The problems with these two is that with the prior election the Moon Sign Ruler was cadent, and in the latter Mars had entered the final two degrees of the Sign. The MSR being cadent allows for success at the start but a bad ending; to me, short term goals were more suited for this election. The final two degrees of a Sign are seen as treacherous and unstable, but some sources believe it is so because these tend to be the Terms of the Malefics. I tend to think it's merely because essential dignity is likely to change, and even if not the element and mode will naturally change because they are never contiguous between Signs.

The setup for the petitions were the standard kit, now augmented by a red silk head covering. I wore red camo pants with a red belt, a Hawaiian style shirt with flames, a steel pendant with a winged sword around my neck along with my new stinger pendant, a bronze raven skull ring, and a red cap over the red silk cloth. I carried a my old M.C. dirk in the left hand, and a steak knife and an ice pick in the right along with the petitional text. (Normally I include multiple handguns but I just wasn't in the mood to dig for them.) All of these are adaptions for the requirements of the petitional instructions.

The real problem was the suffumigation. One is to take wormwood, aloes, squill, spurge, long pepper, and watercress in equal proportions and mix them with human blood.

Spurge was a problem, because I'd run out and my source had evaporated. What I ended up doing was buying an entire plant and harvesting as many leaves as possible without killing the plant itself, which threw the proportions off a little and made the mix harder to burn because of the moisture left in the leaves.

Finally, I tried to obtain the human blood from myself with a syringe completely unsuccessfully and then pricked my fingers a few times with a lancet and dripped that into tissue paper. I am a little squeamish and would make a terrible phlebotomist. I could have predicted what was to happen– by "accident" I had a minor injury a few hours before the second petition and was able to use tissues to soak up some extra blood to augment the mix. (Mars gets thirsty, and things happen.)

Normally, the use of your own blood is a risky proposition in magic and you need to know exactly what the spirits are going to do with it. But in petitions, use of your own blood seems to be safe.

I engaged in planetary dieting for both petitions. I took some canned chili and added additional chili spices until it became almost inedible. But that's the price you pay for power; a lot of Pepto-Bismol in the aftermath.

The first petition was used for vengeance on behalf of two recipients, and the second petition was for health, protection, and victory for several more recipients. The petitional texts needed some modifications for modernization ("king" needed to be substituted with "government" for example), plural tenses, and things like that.

I recited the first petition four times and the latter five, and I would have done the latter many more times except that the stench from the burning blood started to make me cough uncontrollably. I had been wondering if it had been enough blood to satisfy Mars, but damn that stinks so it was probably enough.

The sacrifice listed was a leopard, or a mouse as a fallback. Unfortunately I'm obliged to eat the mouse's liver, so I'm still trying to figure out a third option because that does not seem terribly safe even if overcooked.

Lastly, I do realize that the first chart is without Daylight Savings Time; I adjusted that mentally. I had elected the first one several weeks back, and the second petition was a more recent discovery.

I have seen a lot of people freaking out about having significators in cadent houses.

The rationale of a petition is that you are represented by L1, not primarily the Ascendant itself. Which means that if the L1 is aspecting the petitioned planet, it's not functionally cadent through chart rotation.

As long as L1 and the petitioned planet can "see" each other, it should work. And they can, because you need to have an applying trine or sextile between them.

One of the scourges of the popularity of Astrological Magic is that everyone is trying to elect haircuts and making meatloaf as if they were making talismans. Crafting talismans are only one type of elected Astrological Magic, and most elections are not magical at all.

Chapter Three

Sun Talismans

The Ring of Triumphing Light

Sun 1
Event
Aug 9 2015, Sun
6:05 AM EDT +4:00
Holy Name Hospital
Geocentric
Tropical
Alcabitius

Sun in Domicile Ascending, Moon applying perfected sextile to the Sun, Fortunes in the 1st House

This was a particularly meaningful and powerful election, made in the hours immediately before my mother's gravestone unveiling ceremony, one day after the third anniversary of her death. Her epitaph was, "She was like the Sun; overflowing with beauty, warmth, and bringing cheer. By night unseen, yet not truly gone." I'd often associated her with Solar virtues, which were strong in her nativity; in a way this was a way of honoring her as well as making ten rings of great power.

The Sun Ascends in domicile during Sun Hour and Day. The Moon applies a perfected sextile to the Sun. Though not combust, both Fortunes are in the 1st House. The Sun is never afflicted by planets he is conjoining to, if they are otherwise fortunate. The Moon is fast and in a very fortunate Mansion, and unafflicted. The Moon is angular, and the ruler of his Sign on the 2nd House cusp, just perhaps suggesting a manifestation through wealth.

The main difficulty of the election was that Venus was retrograde and entered 8 degrees of the Ascendant within about nine minutes of the election's commencement. Thus, petition and all ten rings had to be inscribed within this narrow window of time. Having a retrograde planet on the Ascendant (or Ruling it) nullifies an election, though Benefics are more moderate in their afflictions. Two of the final rings were made just barely outside of the window but are probably valid, if weaker.

On this occasion I had an assistant, Jennifer–also my editor and close friend. She made but one of the rings, but mostly fed the suffumigation incense onto the coal and saved me time thereby. I aimed to have her become familiar with my procedures for writing projects in the future.

The materials were selected through divination. The herbal matrix under the rings were celendine and lignum aloes. From this one might assume the rings will combine the protective virtues of celendine with the wealthy virtues of lignum aloes. (Perhaps it will protect against money jinxes? It's impossible to know until one tests it.) The suffumigation was a blend of frankincense, calamus, marjoram, and rosemary. The stones were all bloodstone, and the band was gold wire with a tougher core of gold-plated brass.

The inscription was the word SUN over the Latin *Picatrix* Sun sigil (the one which looks like an inverted V with circular serifs) and the sigil of the Intelligence of the Sun at the bottom- the version with a serif and a circle termination. The smaller rings only used the Latin *Picatrix* sigil. This was also determined through divination.

Aside from running out of time with the 8a (my own notation) everything went splendidly.

All ten of the rings are untouched and pristine and may be bestowed on others, though I probably will claim some for myself at a later point.

Below, I include the highly abbreviated *Picatrix* Solar petition used. Credit me with the edit if you use it anywhere.

"May God bless you, Sun, you who are fortunate and the greater fortune, hot and dry, luminous, resplendent, noble, beautiful, exalted, and honored king over all the stars and planets. Power of beauty, subtlety, good disposition, truth, wisdom, knowledge and riches, which by your virtue are acquired, and in you are made strong. You are the lord of the six planets, which are governed by your motion, and you reign over them and have kingship and lordship over them, and they are obedient to you and depend on your aspect. You are king, and they are vassals. No one can possibly perceive all your good and noble qualities, which are infinite to our intellects. Infuse your spirit and light into these mighty talismans, so that the marvels I desire may be accomplished."

I made a peridot Sun talisman with mule hair for the easing of breathing difficulties (as per Agrippa) for my mother some years ago. It was the only jewelry on her when she died, and I still carry it with me wherever I go.

Let the light shine on!

The Great Ring of Wealth: Marxois

Sun 2
Event
Jan 19 2014, Sun
7:21 AM EST +5:00
Holy Name Hospital
Geocentric
Tropical
Alcabitius

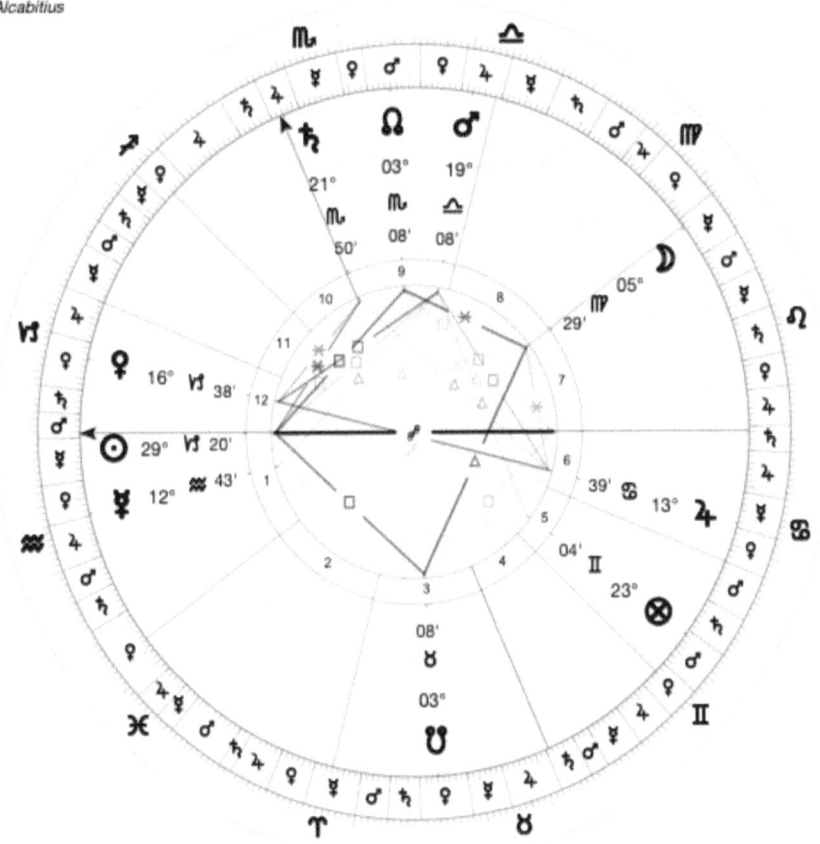

"There rises in the third face of Capricorn a man holding a book which he opens and closes, and before him is the tail of a fish. This is a face of wealth and the accumulation of money and increase and embarking on trade and pressing on to a good end."

It's rare to find a talisman which *just* brings great riches, so this was one I've been hankering to try for a very long time.

Marxois is empowered by the Sun, and the Sun is in the Face in question. Sun is unafflicted. Sun Day and Hour. The Moon is sufficiently fast and widely applying to both benefics by benevolent aspects. The Moon is in her House and conjunct the Pars Fortuna.

The main downside of this election is that it is the final degree of a Sign, but as this is Capricorn and the final degrees of Signs get that reputation largely because of Saturn this may not be as great a concern as otherwise. Furthermore, this election is hard to obtain so one must not demand flawlessness. Saturn is on the MC, but I don't think that'll cause mischief here.

I chose lemon chrysoprase for the stone, and bands made of both gold and gold-filled wire for strength. The suffumigation was long pepper, as was the herb affixed beneath the rings. The oil used was Money Drawing.

Seven rings were made for me, and one undesignated recipient in Size 8.5.

The image of Marxois bears some scrutiny. The Sun is accorded large books according to *Picatrix*, and the figure is of a merlad (a male mermaid) reading a book. This is a way of transmitting that the Sun is in the tail of Capricorn pictorially. In my design, I inscribed MARXOIS across the chest of the figure, and when possible the sigil of Marxois on the binding of the book. The design isn't going to hang in a museum, but it doesn't have to in order for it to work. It also wise to remind oneself that each entry on the Faces in *Picatrix* says "This is its Form." I don't think that word choice is accidental.

It should be noted that *Picatrix* is one of the few sources which consider this a thoroughly positive Face. Most of the others say it inspires selfishness and avarice. I trust *Picatrix* over those sources, but think those may be valid for malefic elections of this Face.

The Ring of Liberation

Sun in Leo

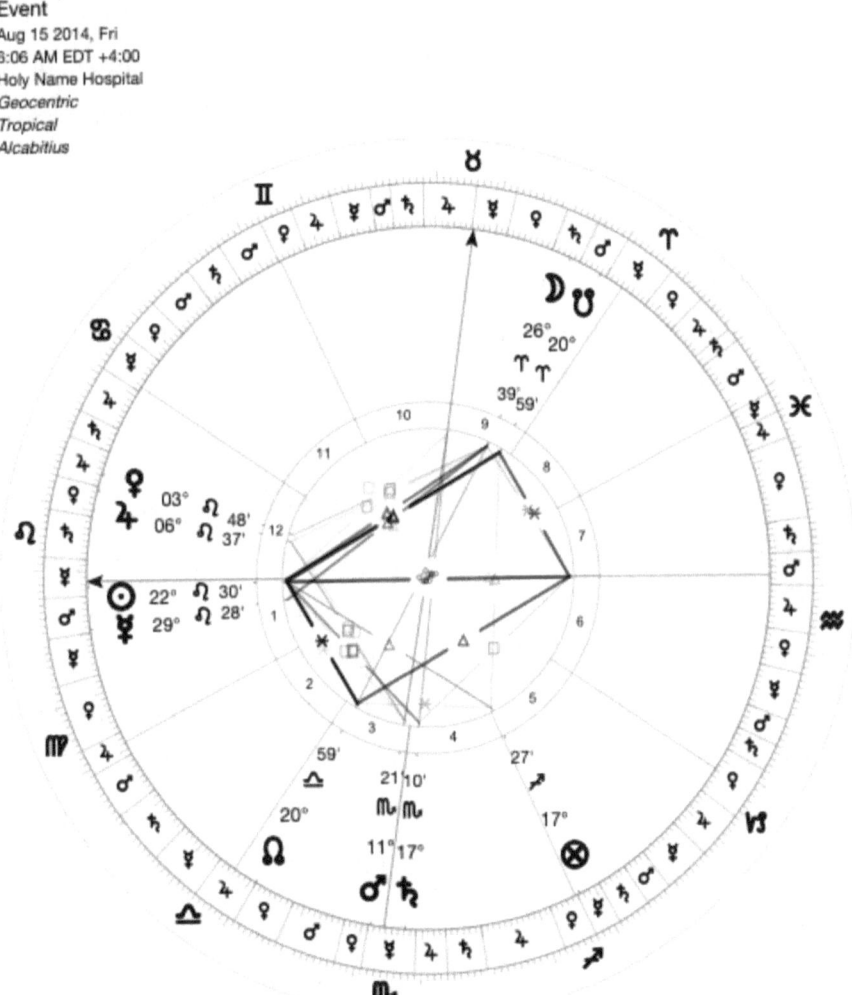

This is a good solid Sun talisman, which I make every year.

Sun Day but not Sun Hour, planet in domicile but not triplicity, Moon fast and unafflicted though cadent, Sun unafflicted. The Moon's Sign Ruler is cadent as well, and normally I'd deem this a problem but the role of the Moon is diminished in Solar elections.

I tend to think that dignity by exaltation allows the user of a talisman to embody the planet's strengths, whereas dignity by rulership gives the user sway over people in any way signified by that planet. This is why it's entirely reasonable to me to double up on exaltation and rulership planetary talismans, and why sometimes one is much preferred over the other.

I particularly find that Sun Rulership talismans have the property of swaying petty bureaucrats, cops, and other people who otherwise might lord over you like a king, to your cause and needs. Self-appointed tyrants are dethroned and made your comrade, with no effort at all.

I was able to test this promptly by breezing through the lines at the DMV three times in one day, even starting out quite late- shortly after making this batch of rings. Around here, one normally expects to spend several hours in line- I burned through the line in about twenty minutes each time. (On two occasions they asked for documents which I didn't have on hand and hadn't realized I needed.) Sun Leo talismans have also gotten me out of situations with cops looking to collect a fine, with utter ease. I have many other examples.

The construction of the rings (there were several) were lemon chrysoprases and bloodstones in gold and gold-filled wire settings.

The suffumigation was gentian, and marjoram was the herb affixed beneath the stone. The oil was Luckymojo.com Sun Oil. Rather atypically, I selected to engrave the Eye of Horus along with the word SUN. The symbol of the Sun is a highly abstracted eyeball, and the Egyptian flavor makes it both historically strong and a bit more pictorial.

A very successful project.

J.R.R. Tolkien's One Ring to Rule Them All

The most famous magical ring in the past century is without a doubt a fictional one; Sauron's ring in Tolkien's popular Middle Earth series, starting with *The Hobbit,* and then *The Lord of the Rings* trilogy. If you haven't read the books you've probably seen the movies, or at least the trailers.

Tolkien based this artifact and plot device on several legends of magical rings from different cultures, but there is some circumstantial evidence that a hitherto undiscovered influence comes from the canon of Scholastic Image Magic which Tolkien would have been familiar with; directly or indirectly, through close colleagues.

It has been an ambition of mine to create a series of rings using the formula that probably inspired Tolkien, and this is the first of a sequence of blog entries which will cover my creation of two sets of rings of this type and a third which is closely related and was created along with the second and arguably superior election.

Tolkien's notion of The One Ring and similar magical artifacts evolved over time, so that Gollum's lost "precious" ring of invisibility is portrayed differently than in The Lord of the Rings trilogy. It evolved from a simple ring of invisibility to an intelligent shapeshifting talismanic repository of the spirit of the dark lord Sauron; capable of making the wearer mighty and swaying nations, extending life in a variety of unnatural manners, and revealing a shadow plane where monsters dwelt. It also had the power to command the wearers of lesser rings whose manufacture Sauron had perverted, most memorably those which belonged to the nine Nazgûl, or Ringwraiths. It is clear that he drew from numerous mythic and fictional sources for its powers and origins, two of which deserve some special attention.

The nigh-archetypical ring of invisibility appears in Plato's *Republic*, where the story of an ancestor of Gyges, a Lydian shepherd, is recounted. In the midst of a discussion about justice and incentives, Plato's brother Glaucon tells a story of how in the absence of accountability both normally good and bad people would choose to behave unjustly. While tending his flock, the anonymous shepherd discovered a tomb in a mountainside after a violent thunderstorm had opened a chasm. In it he found a bronze sarcophagus in the shape of a horse, which when opened revealed a body of a giant with a golden ring on its finger. He took the ring as a prize, and later discovered that when he turned the collet towards his palm he became unseen, and when facing it outward he became visible again. In short order, he exploited this power to seduce the queen and usurp the king and establish a great dynasty of his own. In this story we see for the first time a ring that endows invisibility and rulership; however, the rulership here is described as an unfolding of the abuse of the ring's power rather than a power in and of itself. The ring has some kind of signet or gem, unlike Sauron's ring.

Another obvious influence comes from Wagner's *Der Ring des Nibelungen.* In this cycle of music dramas, a villainous dwarf named Alberich steals gold from the Rhine maidens and crafts it into a magic ring with the power to rule the world. Gods, giants and heroes fight over the possession of the ring for the rest of the story leading to epic tragedies, until escalating mayhem finally leads to the destruction of Valhalla and the death of all of the gods. The conflict on a cosmic scale definitely echoes *The Lord of the Rings.* The ring itself does not have the power of invisibility, but the cycle is based somewhat loosely on the Middle High German text the *Nibelungenleid* where a cloak of great might and invisibility is a plot element and the fate of an (unenchanted) ring leads to the tragic death of many heroes. However, reminiscent of Sauron's ring, the power of Alberich's ring in Wagner comes from rune-magic or taufr, which is sometimes translated as talisman. When touched by flame, Sauron's ring reveals a verse in the language of Mordor describing the powers of the ring. "One Ring to rule them all, One Ring to find them; One Ring to bring them all and in the darkness bind them." Though this verse does not endow the ring with power, it is conspicuous to its appearance. Certainly, the ring of power in *Der Ring des Nibelungen* looks a lot more like Tolkien's ring than the one in Plato. Mystical inscriptions are important; in Plato they are absent.

An additional inspiration which I believe has been overlooked are the instructions for a magical ring suspiciously similar to Tolkien's fictive talisman in one of the most influential books of magic in history; *Three Books of Occult Philosophy* of Henry Cornelius Agrippa, in a chapter on the things falling under the hierarchy of the Sun. One reason why it has been overlooked is that the widespread translation from Latin into English by the anonymous J.F. in 1651 is fairly bad, and uses antiquated English that is hard for modern readers to penetrate.

First, here is the passage in the popular translation:

"Also the Stone Heliotropion green like the Jasper, or Emrald, beset with red specks, makes a man constant, renowned, and famous, also it conduceth to long life: And the vertue of it indeed is most wonderfull upon the beams of the Sun, which it is said to turn into blood, to appear of the colour of blood, as if the Sun were eclypsed, viz. When it is joyned to the juice of a Hearb of the same name, and be put into a vessell of Water: There is also another vertue of it more wonderfull, and that is upon the eyes of men, whose sight it doth so dim, and dazel, that it doth not suffer him that carries it to see it, & this it doth not do without the help of the Hearb of the same name, which also is called Heliotropium, following the Sun. These vertues doth Albertus Magnus, and William of Paris confirm in their writings."

A few years ago, my friend Eric Purdue completed a new translation of Agrippa from Latin to remedy the shortcomings of the J.F. translation and document all of its sources. Here is the new, clearer version of the relevant passage:

"Likewise the stone heliotrope, green in the manner of jasper or emerald with starry red drops, makes one constant, glorious and famous, and brings long life. It also has a wonderful virtue that if it is in the Sun's rays, it is said to change into blood; that is, it appears to be like blood as if the Sun suffered an eclipse—evidently when it is anointed with the juice of the herb of the same name and is placed in a vessel of water filled with water. There is another more wonderful virtue in the eyes of men, which offends the sight and blinds the vision so that it will not permit men to see those who bear it; yet it doesn't happen without the help of the herb of the same name, which is also called heliotrope, that is, following the Sun. These virtues are confirmed in the writings of Albertus Magnus and William of Auvergne."

In the new translation of Agrippa, it is far clearer that this recipe for a talisman endows three powers which seldom coincide in any literature; the power of rulership, longevity, and invisibility.

Most of the properties listed originally come from Pliny the Elder's *The Natural History* including its pairing with the herb of the same name. The associations with it preserving health and youth come from Damigeron in his *De Virtutibus Lapidum*. This stone's power of invisibility is cited later in Boccaccio's *Decameron*. It all comes together in Agrippa.

Within the context of Agrippa, it is strongly implied that the gemstone's power is especially activated if made into an elected astrological talisman. If made into a magical ring, the band would naturally be made of gold; the metal with the greatest sympathy to the Sun.

In spite of featuring a gemstone, this magical ring would otherwise be such a close match for Sauron's ring that it cannot be a coincidence.

The next question is whether J.R.R. Tolkien would have been familiar with the writings of Cornelius Agrippa. He probably was, but he may not have needed to. He was a member of a prestigious

Oxford literary society called the Inklings, devoted to the popularization of fantasy literature. What made this group interesting in our context is that at least three of its prominent members were either practicing magicians or were deeply invested in the literature of Neoplatonic magic. Charles Williams, C.S. Lewis, and Evelyn Underhill would all have been familiar with Agrippa—possibly even the Latin version- and probably would have cited the passage to Tolkien if he had not already found it himself.

Now that we have established that the Solar talisman in Agrippa is a close match for Sauron's ring, we have to dig into the details in order to discern how it might be created in real life.

It has been a long-standing fascination of mine to attempt to reconstruct magics from ancient times which have spectacular, even miraculous effects. I believe that there are many reasons why modern magic seldom produces radical transformations and manifestations, like turning lead into gold, flying carpets, monstrous apparitions, and changes of form. Generally, it is because a number of key elements in the practice of magic degenerated or were hastily purged from the practice of magic from the Renaissance on to the Industrial Revolution. One of the most conspicuous deletions was the usage of traditional electional astrology, and another was the emphasis on the occult properties of herbal, mineral and animal materials. This experiment attempts to restore two of these components in a harmonious and highly intriguing way.

Most scholars agree that the stone Agrippa refers to is modern bloodstone. It is a green jasper with red spots that resemble blood. What is more contentious is the herb; there is a variety of flower called heliotrope today, but Claude Lecouteax believes it corresponds to modern chicory in his *Lapidary of Sacred Stones*—without explaining his rationale in detail. In the *Quindecim Stellis*, heliotrope flowers are an ingredient in talismans of Procyon while chicory is an ingredient in talismans of Alkaid. They are distinct. This compact grimoire is roughly from the fifteenth century and is probably from England; it precedes Agrippa by at least a generation. It's not absolutely clear what herb Pliny the Elder meant, but Agrippa probably believed it was modern heliotrope and not chicory.

That is fortunate for me, being that I recently grew and harvested a bag full of dried heliotrope flowers for my Procyon rings and had quite a bit left over. When reading this passage in Agrippa a few months ago, I realized that I could easily obtain the materials required for the creation of these talismanic rings, and set forth to seek viable elections. I found two.

First Sun in Aries Talismanic Election

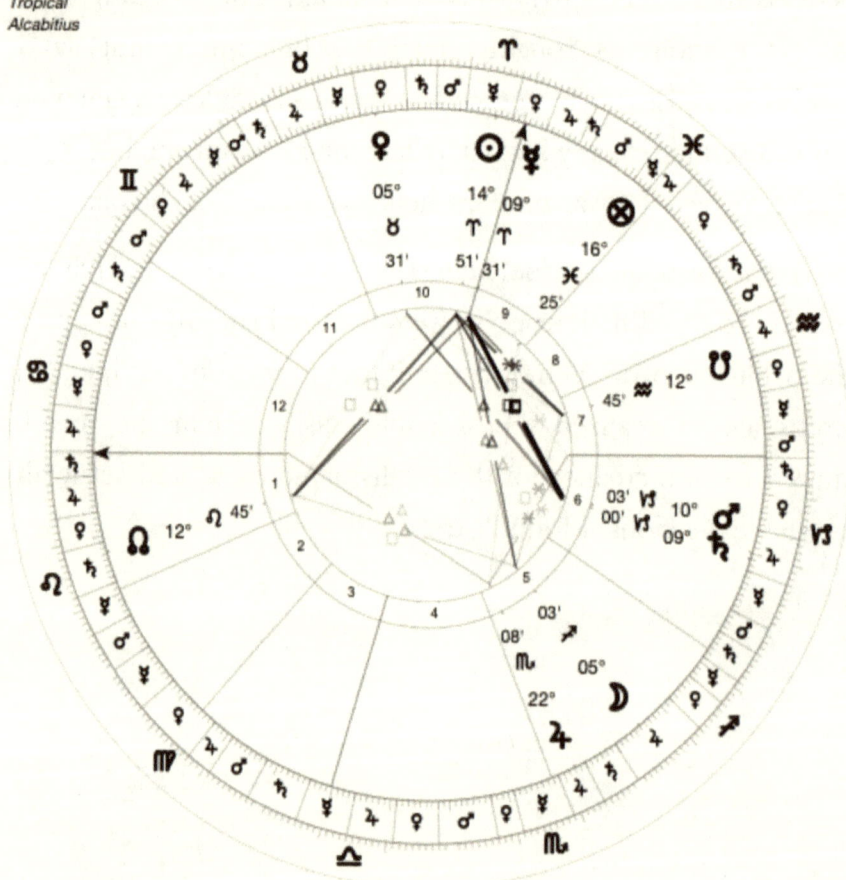

The first election on April 4, 2018 featured the Sun in exaltation in Aries, which is the preferred configuration for fame and elevation into high honors according to *Picatrix*. There hasn't been a good one in several years, and I've definitely been looking. The Sun was also in triplicity as this was a diurnal election.

The Sun was unafflicted and culminating in his planetary Hour. The Ascendant was Cancer so the Moon served as secondary and tertiary significators. The Moon was slow, but not prohibitively, and applying to a trine of Mercury and a far looser trine with the Sun. The Moon was also in the Fifth House, which is a very favorable House, adding accidental dignity. The Sign of the Moon is her own, so she cannot be cadent and thus render the long term outcome unfortunate.

Four bloodstone rings in gold bands were used, with marjoram and heliotrope flowers glued beneath the cabochon. An image of a baron in a chariot drawn by four horses, holding a mirror in the right hand and a shield in the left, was selected from *Picatrix*. The suffumigation was cloves. The smallest ring provided too little surface area for the baronial image, so I used the sigils of the Sun, the word "SUN" and the sigil of the Intelligence of the Sun (Nakhiel) above the rest. One was claimed for myself and three are available for friends and clients.

Second Sun in Aries Talismanic Election

Sun 5
Event
Apr 13 2018, Fri
6:13 AM EDT +4:00
Holy Name Hospital
Geocentric
Tropical
Alcabitius

The second election on April 13, 2018 featured the Sun in exaltation again, but Ascending before dawn in the Hour of the Sun. The Sun again was unafflicted. The Moon was slow and cadent, but in a configuration that I call "triumphing" that is the reverse of besiegement by the Malefics. The Moon was separating from a sextile of Venus and applying to a trine of Jupiter, strengthening her greatly. Furthermore, the Moon was in Pisces while applying to perfect a trine with Jupiter. *Picatrix* says in Book II chapter 3: "Thus when the lord of the Moon's house regards the Moon by a friendly aspect, even if it is an infortune, it will be favorable for petitions and in all that you wish to do." Even though Jupiter was Retrograde, this configuration is very favorable. The Ruler of the Moon's Sign was angular and not cadent, avoiding a bad outcome. Even though the Sun was not in Triplicity, I believe the Moon's configuration in the second election makes it superior to the first.

It also happened to be my grandmother's birthday, so I paid homage to her spirit before reciting the abbreviated petition to the Sun and engraving. Four bloodstone in gold rings were used. The suffumigation was ginger, and heliotrope flowers and gum mastic were glued underneath the cabochons. Three out of four bloodstone rings were claimed by myself; one will go to a friend or a client. The inscriptions were those of the Intelligence of the Sun Nakhiel over the common sigil of the Sun.

Three additional Solar talismans were made before the electional window closed; two rings and a loose gemstone cabochon.

So, at this point you're probably wondering if I've tested out the rings and seen if they work. I have, at least a little. Merely having dried heliotrope flowers under the cabochon doesn't seem to trigger that effect; chicory juice and rotating the collet have not yet been tested.

What has occurred is that I feel healthier and more vigorous than I have in years, and the analytics show that my online presence is undergoing an incredible spike in attention from all around the world. I don't have an adequate explanation for it other than the ring.

Chapter Four

Venus Talismans

A Venus Petition

Venus 1
Event
May 6 2016, Fri
9:04 AM EDT +4:00
Holy Name Hospital
Geocentric
Tropical
Alcabitius

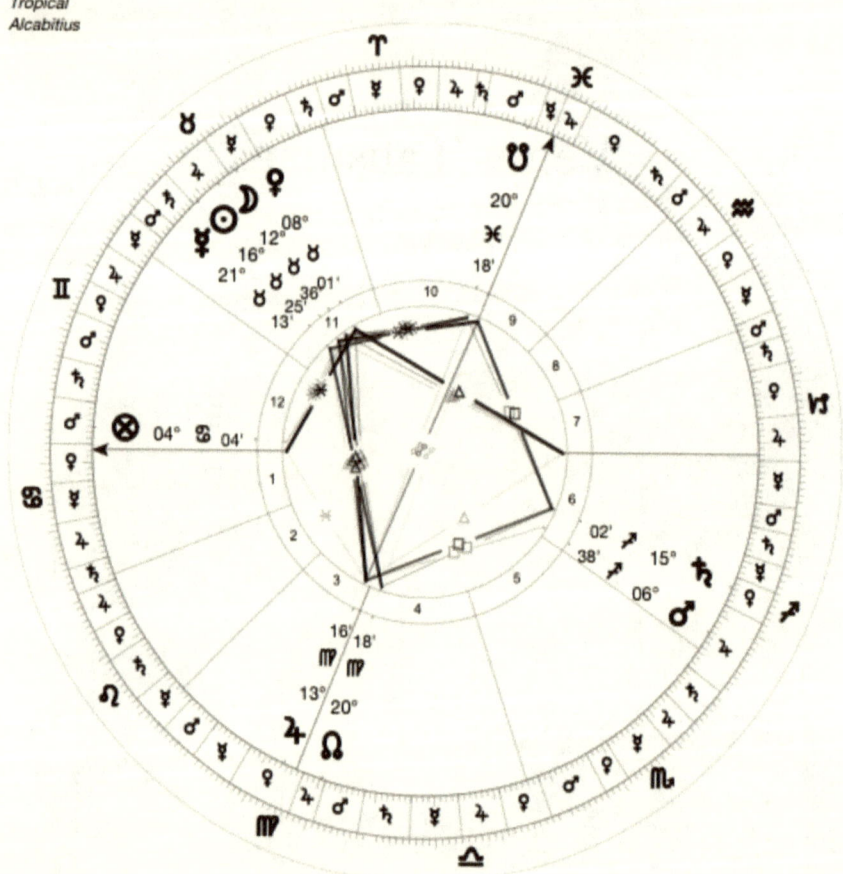

Venus and Moon in Taurus, Cancer ASC, Moon triumphed, Venus sextile ASC

Now, the key with petitions as opposed to talismans is that you're trying to arrange a relationship between the petitioner and the planetary hierarchy in question using the chart. So instead of putting a strong planet on the ASC or MC and thus make the talisman an embodiment of the planetary strength, you make the planet aspect the ASC or ASC ruler in a benevolent manner. This represents assistance rather than embodiment. ASC and ASC Ruler need to be fortified, the planet petitioned needs to be fortified, and the Moon needs to be unafflicted.

This election has Cancer on the ASC and the Moon is exalted, fast, applying in perfection with a Benefic and (arguably) triumphed by "reverse besiegement", protected by combustion in her own Sign, the Ruler of the Moon's Sign is not cadent, and she is in a benevolent succedent House. Venus is very essentially dignified, applying by sextile to the ASC (and Venus loves sextiles more than trines), and is protected by combustion in her own Sign. The pars fortuna is also on the ASC. Day of Venus by both Arab/Jewish and Zoroastrian/Christian planetary days, but not Hour.

The negatives are that the Moon is in fact separating from conjunction with Venus, and one may be concerned about the combustions of Moon and Venus but since both are highly dignified in Taurus and the Sun is also there, it is a good case for these planets shielded by the flames rather than burnt. The 4th Lunar Mansion is not ideal for most matters of Venus, but you can't have everything.

The petition text was taken from *Picatrix*, and I attempted the "dress in the manner of Arabians" option. But only if the Arabs in question were fond of terrycloth bathrobes. I'll hope Venus has a sense of humor about it. I wanted to do more than dress in blue, and I just wasn't feeling like doing a ritual in drag this morning.

The suffumigation listed was gall, frankincense, gum mastic, long pepper, and raisins. I don't have any gall, but I took pomegranate seeds from one of the alternate suffumigation recipes and made do. It was very smoky and I teared up a lot.

"Ask from Venus the desire for copulation, the virtue of causing loves and enthusiasms and expelling sorrow and sloth, invigorating the appetite, increasing generation, multiplying children, extinguishing fire, and being safe from animals."

Magic Rings of Seduction

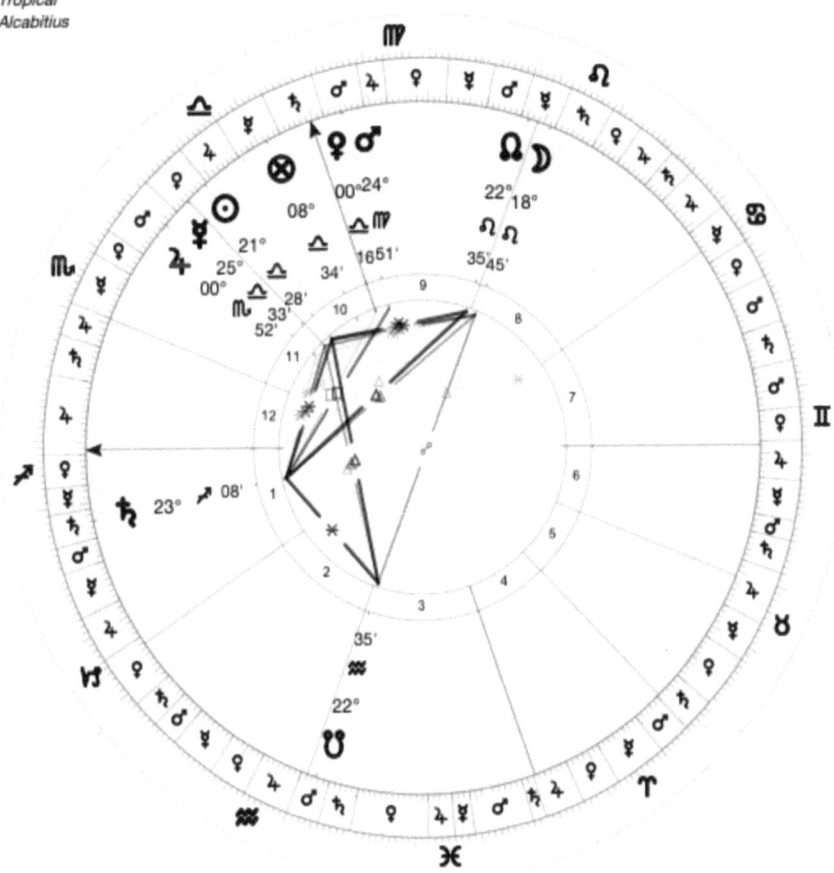

This was a particularly superb election for Venus. So excellent in fact, that I went through some extraordinary efforts and even a few personal sacrifices. What was so good about it to make me jump through flaming hoops?

First, we have Venus in her Rulership in Libra culminating. Not just in Libra, but the first degree of Libra—which is an accidental fortunation in the same way that the final two degrees of any Sign are unfortunate.

Second, the Moon is in a phenomenal state. She is fast, and applying a benevolent aspect to the Ruler of the Sign she is in; something *Picatrix* says is fantastic for any election. She is also applying to conjoin the North Node of the Moon. That's spectacular.

Third, the Ruler of the Ascendant is Jupiter, who while peregrine is in the House of his Joy (the 11th) and in the 1st degree of a Sign. Great accidental dignifications!

There are a few negatives which deserve attention, but no election is perfect. Venus is making no applying aspects. Saturn is in the 1st House and in a malefic decan; but he's not on the Ascendant and Lilly like most Renaissance astrologers deem Saturn to be acceptable in the 1st House generally. It is also Saturn's day, which I feel pays the ferryman off, to an extent.

The Moon is also making a trine to Saturn, and she is waning; something *Picatrix* says reduces the afflictions of the Moon by Saturn. Any aspect to Saturn generally weakens a planet, however. At least Saturn is not retrograde! The waning here is overall positive, because it diminishes the influences of Saturn; especially over time. Lunar phase alone never makes or breaks an election, in my estimation.

Jupiter is under the Sun's Beams but not in combustion. I tend to think this is a moderate affliction. The uncommon positives easily outweigh the less impressive negatives. This election is a juggernaut of sexy. Nothing's gonna stop that lady!

Picatrix describes the natural rulership of Venus in this way: "Venus is the source of the power of flavor. And she rules grammar and the art of measuring sound and song. Among languages she has Arabic; among the internal organs, the right nostril, and among internal organs, those that meet in sexual intercourse and project sperm, and the stomach, and those from which come the virtue and flavor in eating and drinking; among religion, Islam; among clothing, all painted clothing; and of professions, all professions of painting and shaping, selling things that smell good, playing instruments that are good to listen to, singing, dancing and making stringed instruments; among flavors, all sweet things that taste good; and of places, place of vice, places in which men seek healing, and in which men dance, and places of cheerfulness where there is singing and speech, and places of ladies and beautiful women, and also places of eating and drinking; and of precious stones, pearls, and of rocks, lapis lazuli and almartach; and of plants, all plants with a good odor like saffron and arhenda, roses and all flowers with a good odor and smell and are pleasant to look at; among medicines balsam and grains of julep, and those that emit a strong smell, such as nutmeg and amber; among animals, females, camels that are beautiful and all beautiful animals with symmetrical bodies such as gazelles, sheep, gazelles, hares, partridges, calandras and the like. Among small animals, she has those that are colorful and beautiful; among colors, sky blue and gold tending a little to green."

One of the emphases in *Picatrix* which is often less clear elsewhere is that Venus governs music and song in particular. This is why sometimes on talismanic images, Venus is depicted as having the head of a bird, because birds sing.

A similar but perhaps more interesting section appears elsewhere in the text:

"Venus is cold and moist, and a fortune. She signifies cleanliness, splendor, preciousness, word games, delight in music, joy, adornments, laughter, pictures, beauty, loveliness, playing music by the voice or stringed instruments; delighting in marriage, desiring spices and things that have good odors; sending dreams; provoking games of chess and dice; desiring to lie with women and to fall in love with them and receiving promises from them; desiring to appear beautiful, loving liberty, magnanimity of heart, and joy. She abhors anger, brawling, vengeance, and lawsuits; she desires to serve the desires and wills of friends concerning the world's opinion; tends toward false promises; is inclined to cupidity; desires to drink much; incessantly desires much copulation, and of shameful kinds, and to do it in inappropriate places, as women are accustomed to do with one another; delighting in animals and children and in making them good; making things equal; delighting in merchants and living with them and being loved by their women; and that they may be delighted by men. When she is well received, she plays a part in the making of crowns, building stables and working in stone, having sweet speech, disdaining the world and having no fear of it; sustaining people so that neither anger, strife, or discord can be felt by them; it designates a weak heart and a weak will in lawsuits and combat, and signifies desire for all beautiful combinations of things which may be in conformity with the will; making colors and laboring diligently in skills involving them; selling merchandise, spices, and prayers; those who observe the religious law; and those who adhere to sciences and philosophies of forbidden kinds."

One of the differences in the latter section is that it includes several negative attributes, or attributes which we today might considered not complimentary. This is at least partially because this is a description of Venus in general, and not solely when she is essentially dignified; the state which is a common requirement for the production of her talismans.

However, there is a distinction made between what a celestial hierarchy governs, and what it is most suited for in talismans and petitions.

Picatrix gives a fairly wide range of recipes for Venus talismans, including one to make the wearer well-liked by all, one to be always cheerful and happy (basically magical Prozac), one which cures venomous snake bites, one to seduce young men, one which provides immunity from harm, one for general luck and profit, one to drive away mice, one to drive away flies, one to drive away leeches, one to attract the love of women, one to cure children of boils, and one to cure all stomach ailments; and that's just in Book II chapter 10!

What we can derive from this is that Venus is one of the most versatile of planets, capable of bringing many of the pleasures of life, and relieving many of the dangers and annoyances. Venus is always about pleasures and comforts. The only reason why she's deemed the Lesser Benefic is that the Platonists tended toward Stoicism, and favored intellectual joys over the worldly ones.

One of the reasons why we have so many recipes for Venus configurations is that they do help focus the power on particular goals, to the diminishment of other powers. But *Picatrix* does say that if one must choose between a generalized power or a particular power, the former is better. It can be used for many more things, and improve life overall. This is why in the end I used a talismanic design inspired more by Cornelius Agrippa's work than that of *Picatrix*, though there is clear influence from the latter.

Picatrix says in Book III:7: "Seek from Venus all things that pertain to her, such as petitions of women, boys, and girls, daughters, and generally everything pertaining to the love of women and carnal copulation with them, art, vocal and instrumental music, telling jokes, and all those who give themselves over to worldly pleasures, those who engage in vices, male and female servants, brides and grooms, mothers, friends, sisters, and all those similar to them, and in these petitions you may also help yourself with Mars.

I would identify these as the main properties of generalized Venus talismans, as well as guidelines for the optimal requests in Venus petitions."

When indecisive about what to put on a talisman I often inquire with tarot. Sometimes the size and shape of the material limit the choices, and sometimes time restricts options when you're creating several talismans in a narrow electional window.

Since this project was a series of rings in varying band sizes and gemstone sizes, it would be necessary to use sigils for the smallest only because it is hard to engrave elaborate tableaus on a small cabochon.

There also needs to be enough time during the full electional window to recite at least an abbreviated petitional text, engrave, suffumigate repeatedly, and affix the herbs with glue on all talismans before the time window ends.

The gemstone chosen was carnelian. One of the more unexpected Venereal stones, the gem looks a little like raw meat and even the name is suggestive of carnality and carnivorous; it is not surprising that it is co-ruled by Mars. The band was gold wire wound around a core of gold-filled wire to strengthen it. Gold and bronze are both suitable metals for Venus.

The herbs under the ring were thyme and vervain—both Venereal. Thyme is a love herb, and vervain has associations with bewitchment and in particular the power of fascination.

All in all, it's a material expression of sexual desire in the language of herbs and stones.

The suffumigation was storax. I almost went with balsam, which is also a good choice. I used that in another recent election. I really do love the sexy scent of storax. (I get mine from Alchemy Works .)

The image was as depicted; the sigil of the Intelligence of Venus, Hagiel, at the center. Below was the word Venus, and at the top was the Venus sigil variant from the Arabic *Picatrix* (the Ouroboros Press version). The Latin *Picatrix* sigil is taller and the triangle is smaller, but is otherwise the same. I like it because it's a little mysterious and weird, and not recognizable to people who haven't studied SIM.

The planetary Intelligence is often used in tandem with a planetary Spirit. Unfortunately, there is some ambiguity whether planetary Spirits are simply lower order daimones, or actual evil demons. Agrippa is a bit confusing on the matter. In any case, I do not work with demonic beings for any reason, and my Venus talismans seem to work fantastically without the sigil of Kedemel (the Venereal planetary Spirit).

I believe that the planetary Intelligences are a class of beings not from the planetary spheres, but who control the affairs of those realms from afar in the uppermost cosmic sphere (either the 9th or 10th, depending on the model you use). This gives them lofty power, but will behave in a somewhat fickle and arbitrary manner at times, because they are quite alien and godlike. There are many interesting things to be learned about them when you compare what Agrippa writes and their origins in the work of Pseudo-Dionysius the Aeropagite. If I am correct, planetary Intelligences are supercelestial and thus they can magnify the power of any elections which fall under their governance.

Seven rings were created, one of which has already been delivered to a client. I will surely keep at least a couple for myself. This was a great project to work on.

The Ring of Dragonfire's Kiss

The talisman of Venus in Libra, embraced by the Sun and conjoined with the Dragon's Head

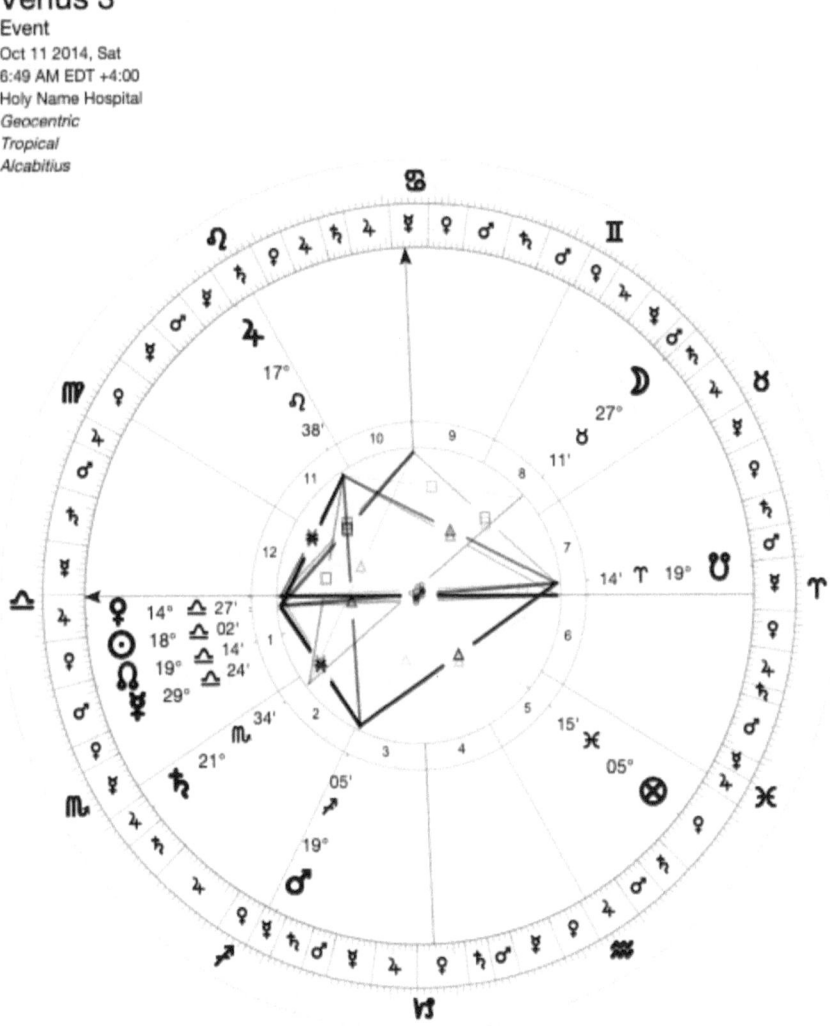

This was one hell of an experimental election. It's one of the potentially strongest Venus elections possible masquerading as one of the worst.

Let's start with the basics. Venus Day but not Hour, Ascending, in Domicile. The Moon is fast, in Triplicity and Exaltation, towards the end of a Sign but not quite in the last two degrees. (Also in a malefic House, but I don't see this as a significant consideration here. A benefic on the ASC rectifies an afflicted Moon anyway.) Venus is also fairly tightly conjoined with the North Node, radically strengthening her.

The main objective for this election was to put Venus in conjunction with the North Node and strong Essential Dignity, which is not easily achievable.

There's just one problem: Venus is combust. Most people would stop here, but the story isn't over. Venus isn't combust in just any Sign, but both planets are in Venus' Domicile. Ancient sources suggest that this either neutralizes the afflictive nature of the combustion, or actually is a strong accidental dignity.

I take the view currently that while combustion is normally akin to a subject trembling before a king, begging for mercy, this is like the king visiting a beloved vassal in their estate to pay him a great honor and treat him almost as an equal.

Even if we accept this interpretation, there is another problem- and it's a tough one. While Venus is in +5 Rulership, the Sun is in -4 Fall. Does this mean the king is a lousy houseguest? Is this hostility? Most sources are ambiguous on the issue. *Picatrix* is not.

It's too long to quote here, but in *Picatrix Rubeus* pages 90-91 the author says that when planets are in conjunction, the higher planet dominates the union and it is its nature which is signified thereby- with a few notable exceptions. That means normally when the Moon conjoins Saturn, the latter's nature wholly devours the influence of the Moon. Nothing of the Moon's significance remains, except as fuel for the nastiness of Saturn. This pattern is the case for all planets, where the naturally slower (higher) planet absorbs the power of the naturally slower one.

The exceptions appear to be conjunctions of Jupiter and Saturn, which are roughly co-equal; and Mars and Saturn, where Mars will dominate the union. A third exception is when the lower planet is highly dignified AND the higher planet is highly debilitated. Then the lower planet dominates the conjunction and incorporates the power of the greater planet. That is what is happening here, where Venus is extremely strong and the Sun is extremely weak. So, Venus easily wins the struggle with the Sun, in part because it's on her home turf.

I often say, conjunction is fighting or fucking. With Venus... it's *really* not fighting. She's lured the king to her palace (or brothel), tied him to the bedposts and worn the poor guy out. She's the king now, in everything but title. He can barely lift his head. Everything aches. But don't worry about him, he'll get a second wind in Scorpio. And he had a great time with Mistress V.

There are other factors which should be noted. Venus is making a sextile with Mars, but as this is an amicable aspect and Venus is one of the very few planets which gets along with Mars, it's not a serious affliction. The Moon being v/c is never a real problem. It's a minor consideration, even in Mansion talismans. Even so, it's not deemed an affliction at all according to Bonatti if the Moon is also in any Essential Dignity, which it is here. And Lilly made a separate list of

Signs where v/c is very mild, which overlaps the Bonatti list to a large degree.

In any case, I made three rings. The theme was red; the stone was carnelian, and the herbs under the stone and suffumigation were vervain and saffron. The oil was Luckymojo.com Venus Oil.

The image was of the giant housefly head over the zebra head which cures stomach ailments, though I believe in this instance it will do very different stuff. But a heartburn cure isn't a bad thing, as a bonus.

The Ring of the Kiss of Darkness

Venus in Zero Scorpio, Cazimi

This is the first set of rings I've ever made which could conceivably require a safeword.

I have long theorized that talismans must be possible which go beyond the morality/luck vs immorality/misfortune dichotomy.

Everything in the skies is reflected on Earth and vice versa. So luck with sinful endeavors must be possible to elect, and furthermore imbue into a talisman. So I made myself a triad of rings that shoots perverto-beams.

One method to do this is to use mixed Essential Dignity and Essential Debility. Some consider peregrination to be an intermediate state; I don't. It is a state of powerlessness and inertia, which when combined with Essential Debility results in misfortune and an inability to escape it, as well as poor judgement. But when Essential Debility is combined with any manner of Essential Dignity, the powerlessness of peregrination is annulled, and the Debility represents vice and immoral aims, while Dignity represents power and skill in this sphere of influence. That's how you signify someone who is really good at being really bad.

Venus is in Scorpio, putting her in Detriment. This is a -5 and peregrine by most reckonings. However, though most tables of Essential Dignities and Debilities give Mars both diurnal and nocturnal triplicity for the Watery Signs, some give Venus diurnal Triplicity for Water. This makes much sense to me, as Venus loves moisture, and lending so much power to Mars without balance strikes me to be unreasonable. Thus, Venus receives a +3 through Triplicity, ultimately being a mere -2 tally and escapes peregrination.

Nevertheless, Venus is at 0 Scorpio and that's the heart of the Via Combusta. This election was very, very wicked.

But extremely strong by accidental dignity, because Venus is also firmly in cazimi. She is unified with the dark flame of the Sun in Scorpio. So, Venus is lucky in bad, naughty, no-good, dastardly

Venus matters. And because Venus is in cazimi/combustion, she can do them secretly and nobody will ever know.

What does Lilly say about Venus when ill dignified? "Then he is Riotous, Expensive, wholly given to Loosenesse and Lewd companies of Women, nothing regarding his Reputation, coveting unlawful Beds, Incestuous, an Adulterer; Fennatical, a meer Skipjack, of no Faith, no Repute, no Credit; spending his Means in Alehouses, Taverns, and amongst Scandalous, Loose people; a meen Lazy companion, nothing careful of the the things of this Life, or any thing Religious; a meer Atheist and natural man."

Well, that's just so very judgmental of you, Mr. Lilly. If I ever feel like being wholly given to the lewd companies of women, coveting unlawful beds, and spending excessively in taverns among scandalous, loose people, I know who I won't be inviting to the party. But I know which ring I'll be wearing for the occasion.

I'll also totally get away with it, because a planet under combustion is hidden and escapes scrutiny. And it will come easily because Triplicity signifies ease, and it will be immensely strong because cazimi is pretty mighty.

The traditional literature's description of afflicted Venus is a veritable catalogue of sexual perversion. This is the ring you wear to a dungeon, to prove the Devil himself has dropped by to show them some new tricks. Then, you disappear into the night and people wonder if they imagined the whole thing... This really is the Rock Star Lifestyle ring, except that it's sneaky. I'm okay with that.

In any case, let's break down the rest of the details.

The Moon is combust and in the 1st House and separating from Venus, but afflictions of the Moon are rectified by having a benefic on the ASC or MC. I don't think this is a really big deal, but it must be noted. Venus Day and Hour. Nice. The Moon is in the 17th Mansion, which offers durable loves and friendships. It's not clear if this is a genuine factor. I guess if my newly acquired slaves stick around I can make them do the laundry.

Saturn is in Scorpio, which will weaken the election somewhat, but I do not deem this a significant factor. The Moon is conjoined to the Part of Fortune, but that's normal for a chart of this kind.

Anyway, the inscription on the rings was the bird headed girl holding an apple and comb, with the OAOIOA looking bit. The herbs beneath the ring were violet and thyme, and the suffumigation was violet, thyme, and storax resin. Tarot liked this, but actually wanted storax and myrtle for a suffumigation... but I was all out of myrtle. I need to do better inventory.

Three rings were made: two large carnelian and one medium lapis lazuli.

The oil used was Luckymojo.com Magnet Oil. Magnet Oil has a reputation for powerful influences on money, and lovers which are extreme and somewhat unnatural in character and extent. Considering the flavor of this ring, I knew it wasn't going to be Marriage Oil.

It's probably because they scared me a little from the start that I didn't file them into storage. I didn't particularly relish the prospect of touching them. I had no immediate desire to go barhopping or whatever, so they sat on my computer desk in three little bathroom cups. There they sat for days, and then weeks. There was no way to forget they were there–they had a certain presence, as all ensouled objects do. They did not draw me to them, nor were they particularly repulsive. They sat like sleeping panthers; a sense of possible danger, but only if they awoke hungry or in a foul mood.

I had a sewer line back up into my basement in June, after I'd been making experimental talismans with cazimi and eclipse configurations. The insurance company did offer to pay for the restoration, but I became ambitious and decided to pick the top basement remodelers in the area and create an epic "man cave" to replace what was pretty foul even before the unwelcome arrival of my neighbors' effluvia through the wall. In the intervening months I salvaged and relocated the contents of the basement upstairs, and waited impatiently for my turn in the waiting list of clients.

It was very messy work, dusty, and even after things were technically sterilized, it wreaked havoc with my allergies. My skin itched, my hands swelled, and I began to sneeze until I feared my sore nose would snap off. The result of this was that I became lethargic and sloppy, and my top floor bedroom filled with storage boxes and old medical equipment from the basement, and the floor littered with balled up tissues and dirty laundry. The room was completely unpresentable, even to close friends. Rather than a proper bedroom, it had turned into a cramped cubby for sleeping and sneezing.

A couple of weeks before the basement reconstruction was to begin, there was a torrential rainstorm. In the middle of the night I heard a rhythmic snapping sound, and discovered that rain was dripping through the roof onto an old shopping bag cast into a corner. Droplets hitting the paper bag were making the sound. The roof had actually been damaged during hurricane Sandy, but only now was there obvious leakage. I had a roofer come out to the house and fix it, and paid a hefty amount but still it was less than I expected. I paid in cash to get that discount–a little bit risky, but I had an expensive basement repair fast approaching and I didn't want to be short of funds at any critical juncture.

A couple of weeks later, another big storm blew through my area and the roof began to leak as if no repair had ever been done. I began to panic, because I had paid in cash and thus no official guarantee on the repair. Nevertheless, the roofing company said they'd send someone out over the next few weeks free of charge. I started to relax about it, slightly. A promise is nice, but a contract is more tangible.

It was then that I noticed that my roof had sprung that leak one yard to the left of the three Venus Scorpio rings, barely missing my rickety computer desk. I began to wonder if the rings were sending out their rays and damaging the roof, drawing in the harmful water of Scorpio and the discomfort of moist Venus in her detriment.

No, it was actually much worse than that.

A week after the promise of a second roof repair, my doorbell rang at an ungodly hour (at least for me) and the repairman from before had returned, unannounced. A seemingly recent immigrant from Ireland, his accent was thick and his many tattoos were overflowing with Celtic knotwork and cruciform imagery. I was asleep when he rang, and without obvious cues like that I might not have recognized him.

If I hadn't been so eager to get the roof fixed I might have told him to come back later, except that without a contract I worried he might not actually return–or be offended with the same result.

I slipped on my sandals and shambled outside, trying to show him the part of the gabled roof where I thought the leak originated, but because I was groggy I became less certain of how the roof oriented to the ceiling within, and exasperatedly invited him up to my room to see where the leak came from, trailing muddy sandalprints through my front hallway.

Half awake and a bit woosy, I put no thought to how a fairly conservative blue collar gentleman would react to seeing my bedroom.

He actually played it cool. I have to give him credit.

But from his perspective, he had just been invited into the lair of a devil-worshipping pervert and possible serial killer.

There's pretty much no way he could have come to any other conclusion.

You see, my bedroom is where I keep about a thousand books on the occult and horror fiction. Most of the decorations involve skulls, and creatures with devil horns. It's deliberately designed to be a bit spooky–I collect Balinese masks, for example. The bull skull I have hanging from the rafters is actually a composite Venus Taurus talisman. There's a framed print of an anatomical heart in blue on one wall. The look is for my amusement, and there's normally no reason why someone who would object to these things would ever see them.

The rest of my home isn't very scary looking. He must have felt like he'd entered the anteroom to Hell.

He asked what that red stuff was, seemingly dripping down the walls. I had to tell him that it gets very hot up there in August and the wood stain sometimes melts and then hardens that way. I don't think he believed me. (Under normal circumstances I rather enjoy bragging that my walls bleed.)

Because I tend to sleep late, I have blackout windowshades. To someone who didn't know what they were, they might look like something to conceal a murder. The rags and old clothing on the floor might have looked like they belonged to a victim of a terrible sex crime. The coils of medical tubing and other questionable objects from the basement didn't do much to alter this impression either. God knows what he thought were in those stacked boxes. At least they were clean and dry. But unlabeled.

All on the path leading him to the corner of the room where the leak had sprung. Right next to the three rings...

Where there were now unopened boxes of childrens toys-which I actually use as ancestral offerings. But explaining that probably wasn't going to do much good. I'm sure he was confident it was fresh bait for my next victims.

The proximity of balled up tissues from my constant sneezing probably made the situation a little bit less wholesome. I really hope he missed the box of condoms, but at that point it's just gilding the lily.

He did not spend long at my house, but I'm happy to say the roof has stopped leaking. The police have not stopped by to ask about missing children, either. Geraldo Rivera has not turned up at my door for an interview. All is good.

It may be useful to go back and re-examine what Signfication means and specifically what a *debilitated* Venus signifies.

Signification is about your experience of something in the context of meaning. Flame partakes as much of the element of fire as super hot chili peppers, even if the burning is of a different kind. The fact that the constellations are made of burning balls of gas that may have burned out millions of years ago tells you nothing about why they might look like a turtle and (maybe) foretell the onset of hair loss. (I'm just making that up.) It is your experience and the effects we study, not intermediate mechanisms. The Gods of Time do not micromanage.

Venus fortified is pleasant and leads to happy, socially approved outcomes. Sweet tastes, sweet dreams, healthy sex in the missionary position leading to wedded bliss and 2.5 kids. Or at least the impression of such things. I've actually met some people with extremely strong natal Venus who were outwardly square and a bit boring, but privately were quite peculiar.

Venus afflicted signifies taboos broken, and whatever acts of pleasure are loathed and feared by society at that point in time. It is as much about the reaction of shock and scandal as it is about the act itself–and it is one of the exceptions to the rule that astrology and the heavens themselves are perennial and constant. Standards change; *Picatrix* cites lesbian exhibitionism in a list of Venereal fortitudes, but the manuals of the Renaissance list everything from spanking to necrophilia as afflictions of Venus.

We live in a very jaded era, where Fifty Shades of Taupe has become the very definition of bourgeois sexuality. There are furry fandom conventions and enough of a market to justify several different colors and sizes of tentacle-shaped dildoes. It takes a lot to convey an enormity of sexual depravity and unwholesomeness today.

I think that I have a clearer notion of what might achieve that than I did a few weeks ago. So does my former roofer.

And it happened right in front of those three Venus Scorpio rings, which drew all the pieces together like iron filings to a lodestone. Which is how astrological talismans often work.

I shall also point out that no damage occurred. The only consequences to this so far have been a mild discount on a roof repair and two people probably enjoying telling somewhat divergent accounts of that visit.

The rings are now in a storage box, along with several less dangerous talismans which surely will neutralize their effects to a large degree.

Even in Scorpio, Venus entertains.

(Postscript: These turned out to be so dangerous that they needed to be dropped into the ocean, along with other problematic talismans.)

Chapter Five

Mercury Talismans

The Ring of the Green Lion

Picatrix Rubeus page 109: "If, under the influence of Mercury, you make the image of a lion in emerald... in the hour of Mercury, Mercury rising in Gemini... whoever has this image will evade infirmities and fear, and good things will be said of them."

Mercury 1
Event
May 28 2014, Wed
2:08 PM EDT +4:00
Holy Name Hospital
Geocentric
Tropical
Alcabitius

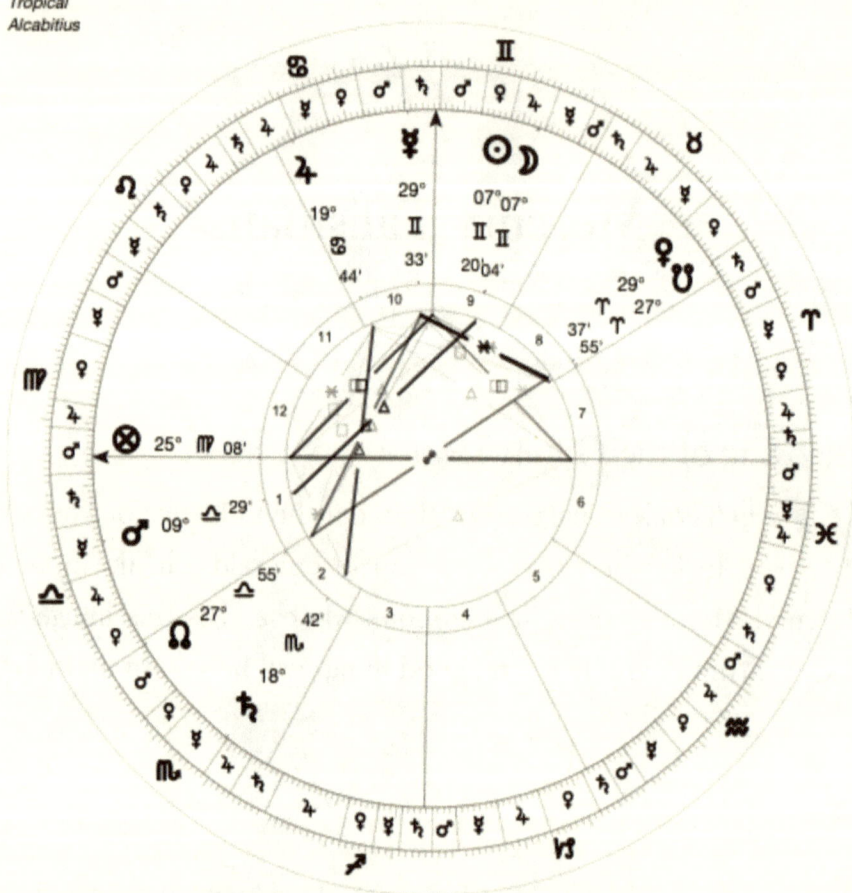

    I think this was an altogether remarkable election, less so for the placement of Mercury but for the Moon.

    Mercury culminates during Mercury Day & Hour, in Domicile, with Virgo on the ASC. The Moon is in cazimi, sufficiently quick, and itself also in Gemini.

    Mercury is slow, at the end of a Sign, and making a fairly wide square of Mars, which I believe will be suppressed by refrenation.

The Moon is applying to a trine of Mars, but as the Moon is still technically waning this is only a tolerable affliction and is easily surpassed by the enormous strength of the cazimi.

Many of the attributes of evasion, confusion, protection, and charm which are the aims of the talisman work well with this particular horoscope configuration. My own divinations strongly supported this hypothesis and now must be put to the test.

Six rings were made of the heavily included emerald and of wire. The suffumigation was caraway seed. The herb beneath the stones was cinquefoil. Luckymojo Mercury Oil was used in the operation.

Talismans of Trust

Extremely dignified Mercury Ascending in Virgo with the North Node, with the Moon applying to a conjunction of Jupiter

Mercury 2
Event
Jul 28 2017, Fri
7:47 AM EDT +4:00
Holy Name Hospital
Geocentric
Tropical
Alcabitius

This project was full of all kinds of surprises, great and slightly bad.

My lost emerald cabochon which popped out of its ring at ConVocation and I'd deemed lost forever was found right before the election taped to the side of a box with packing tape. I've observe that I often lose a talisman when the planet it's based upon is in Fall, and I recover it when it is Exalted. That's seemingly what happened here. My lost Mercury spirit came back home, right on schedule.

And then, about 4/5ths of the way through the electional window– after I'd engraved the images but right before I added the vegetal component–my street had an hour long blackout. So I had to finish the project by candlelight. I did end up adding the herbs to the rings after the planetary hour had ended, but thinking quickly I dipped the rings in a tea of the herb and finished the whole thing before Mercury was fully off the Ascendant. I think it should be fine. Other than that, this was a pretty great election.

Mercury was greatly essentially dignified. In Domicile, Exaltation, and Term. Mercury was making a loose sextile to a Benefic and moving reasonably fast. The Moon was slow but waxing and applying to conjoin with Jupiter (finally Direct and gaining speed.) For the early part of the election, the North Node was on the Ascendant, adding much good fortune. The Moon's Sign Ruler was succedent, which is good. The Moon's Mansion is suitable for works of love and friendship, which seems compatible as well. The electional window was about thirty minutes for engraving, cut off a bit by the end of the planetary hour.

For the larger talismans I chose the *Picatrix* frog acceptability talisman in *Picatrix* II:10.

"If, under the influence of Mercury, you make the figure of a single frog on the hour of Mercury, with Mercury rising, in an emerald stone, whoever carries it will offend no one. To the contrary, everyone you meet will speak well of you and say good things about your works."

"MERCURY" was engraved across the middle of the frog, though in one instance the word was placed on the back.

For the smaller, I used the Latin *Picatrix* Mercury sigil, which resembles the standard Mercury symbol but has a stem between the "horns" and circle, and the lower cruciform portion is slightly squashed.

For the herb below the rings I used aniseed. For suffumigation I used gum arabic, cloves and myrtle. It did not burn terribly easily, but it worked after a few tries.

The incantation was the standard long version of the *Picatrix* Mercury petition.

Six emerald ring talismans in gold wire were made. One additional green agate ring talisman with gold-filled wire was made. One moss agate tie clip talisman was made. Two loose brown agate cabochon talismans were made– brown agates protect against injuries, especially if made into talismans. A pair of very unusual lodestone/magnetite talismanic cufflinks were made. And finally, one large emerald cabochon talisman was made.

Ultimately only the cufflinks got the sigil. The remainder all got the Mercury frog, even the brown agates.

Chapter Six

Moon Talismans

Some Notes on the Operation of the Moon

Page 191: "The Operation of the Moon. When you wish to do the magical works of the Moon, do so when the Sun is in Cancer and the Moon in Aries, which is the exaltation of the Sun, and do the work in the night of the Moon (that is, on Sunday, when the day has ended.)"

Picatrix does appear to use the normal system of Planetary Hours, but Planetary *Days* are different. Following Jewish and Muslim custom, the day begins at nightfall and thus Saturn's day begins Friday night, etc. However, there is no indication that Hours are altered by this.

It does mean that if we are working with *Picatrix* centered elections, workings that require Planetary Day and are nocturnal, need to be scrutinized. At best, this means there are more elections we can use, as we alternate between systems. At worst, we're going to have to decide for ourselves which system works best for us by trial and error.

Rubeus p 127:

"Similarly, you should know that the aspects of the Moon with planets are more powerful when the Moon is oriental of the Sun and in front of him, and not when she is behind him. The aspect of the Moon and the Sun by sextile or trine is good in all high works in which you seek treasure, great wealth, royal power, honor and victory. When in the all of the preceding operations the Moon is in the tenth house, the effects are good and very strong in completing the work, which cannot be when she is in the fourth or seventh houses, nor when the Moon is waning or combust of the Sun."

This is an apparent paradox.

Unless I'm getting my terminology bungled at 9 in the morning, the Moon is waning (by our use of the term) when she is oriental of the Sun, and this is a fortitude with aspects. But only a few lines later, it is asserted that the effects are impaired when the Moon is waning.

Does this mean that effects are strong when aspects are weak? That seems entirely contradictory.

Nope. It's that *Picatrix* uses an uncommon definition of waning.

Rubeus p 71:

"In all your workings... always observe in your workings the waning of the Moon, for when she wanes, it shows and reveals destruction and detriment, slowness and weakness in all things of this world. This is the waning of the Moon: that is, when she decreases by light and the calendar, and is slow in motion."

Which means that two conditions are required for the Moon to be deemed *Picatrix* waning- it must be between Full and New, and also slow (elsewhere, indicated to be under 12 degrees of motion per day.) So, this doesn't happen nearly as much as conventional waning.

There is further evidence for this immediately following.

"The state and condition of the Moon is good when she is increasing by light and the calendar, and swift of course, nor is she regarding Mars by any aspect, because when the waxing Moon beholds Mars, this is considered to be a great affliction of the Moon, and when she beholds Saturn while waxing, this is a grave affliction."

The Moon is harmed more by aspects with malefics while waxing but less while waning. Yet we have tended to assume that the waning moon is a weaker condition- yet it overcomes the malefics in that state. My own experience follows this. The Moon is strongest when she is fast, between Full and New.

Picatrix page 71: "Thus when the lord of the Moon's house regards the Moon by a friendly aspect, even if it is an infortune, it will be favorable for petitions and in all that you wish to do."

This is one of the really great loopholes that nobody notices. I made a talisman with this in effect which otherwise would have been unacceptable.

So, for example, you have the Moon waxing in Capricorn making a sextile to Saturn-that's not a malefic election anymore by any means.

I personally don't have big problems with the Moon in Capricorn and Scorpio unless there's a problematic aspect or the Moon is inarguably in the via combusta. If all else is benevolent, the effect seems to be to slow things down and add a chill to objectives– which is often beneficial.

When the Moon's debility combines with a violent aspect the slowdown is like a poison or strangulation, which is why Lunar essential debilities are used for curses. They create adversity and mire the target in it, so they cannot escape.

The Ring of the Serpent of Healing

The Eighteenth Mansion triumphed, with the North Node Rising

This was somewhat borderline, but I was encouraged by advice from tarot to make six rings of this configuration.

Rubeus page 290 in the Plinian Mansion section: "The eighteenth Mansion is Alcab, and it is for taking away fevers and infirmities of the belly. When the Moon is passing through this Mansion, fashion from wax the image of an adder holding its tail above its head. Suffumigate it with the horn of a stag and say: 'You, Egribel, guard this house of mine that no serpent may enter nor any other hurtful beast.' Place the image in a vessel which should be buried beneath your house; when the aforesaid has been done, then no serpent will be able to enter nor any other hurtful creature. If the image is to relieve a fever or illness of the belly, carry this image with you and it will cure you. Know that Egrebel is the name of the lord of this Mansion."

The main concern of this election was that we just passed an eclipse, and nobody is sure how big the orb of influence of an eclipse is. I think enough time had elapsed, but experimentation is the key to discovery. It was much more time than the last time I made a talisman which got horrible from an eclipse.

The Moon is slow and succedent, which would invalidate the election except for the North Node on the ASC and the Moon enclosed between aspects of the Benefics. The application to Venus is rather wide, but this is not a limit on besiegement so it should not be a limit on triumphs (which is what I'm calling benevolent besiegement these days.) It is also the Moon's Day but not the Hour. The ASC Ruler is highly essentially dignified, but separating from conjunction with Capulus and applying to a wide opposition to a retrograde Saturn. Nevertheless, when a planet or the Nodes are on the ASC, the ASC Ruler becomes a tertiary consideration IMHO.

Not being able to break down my stag horn in time to make a powder suitable for suffumigation, I used licorice root (used to settle stomach problems), and Luckymojo.com's Moon Oil, in combination with amber resin from Alchemy Works.

Six rings with quartz cabochons were prepared, with gold-filled/rolled gold wire (which is basically gold-plated brass.) One for myself, five for friends and future clients.

The image was of a serpent in the configuration of a letter C flipped along the vertical axis, with the head below. The sigil of the North Node was engraved where convenient, and EGRIBEL across the middle of the surface.

Talisman of Safe Driving

Moon culminating triumphed and fast in the 7th Lunar Mansion, Ascendant Ruler fast and dignified

Moon 3
Event
May 26 2017, Fri
2:20 PM EDT +4:00
Holy Name Hospital
Geocentric
Tropical
Alcabitius

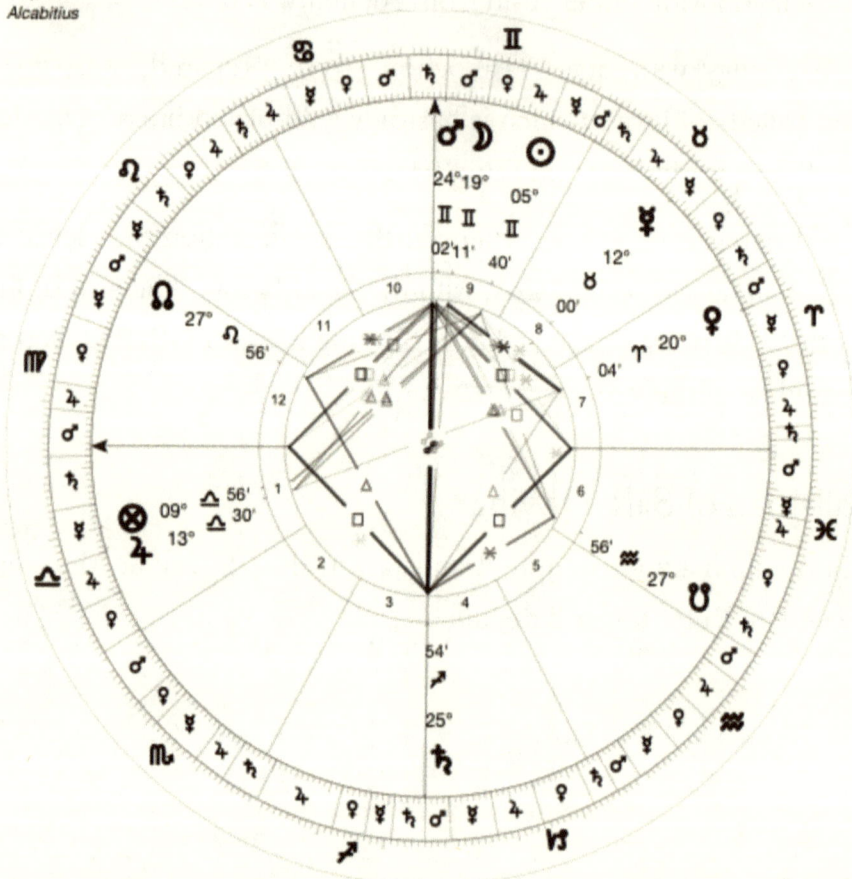

This is a 7th Mansion talismanic election for safe travel, particularly by car.

Picatrix gives the name of the Mansion's ruler as Siely and alternately as Sehele in the Plinian Mansion section, derived from Ibn Hatim: "The seventh Mansion is Aldira and is for the acquisition of all good things. When the Moon is passing through this Mansion, fashion a seal of silver, and sculpt the image of a man clothed in robes and with his hands extended to heaven in the manner of a man who is praying and supplicating; in the breast of the image write the name of the lord of this Mansion. Suffumigate it with sweet smelling things, and say: "You, Siely, cause such and such to happen, and grant my petition." Ask for whatever you wish that pertains to good things. Carry the image with you and it will be as you wish. Know that Selehe is the name of the lord of this Mansion."

Picatrix, however, gives more options for the 7th Mansion in the "foundational" Mansion section much earlier in the book. "The seventh mansion is called Aldirah. 25 It begins at 17 degrees 8 minutes and 36 seconds of Gemini and its boundary is the end of that sign. In this Mansion make images to increase merchandise and profit and to travel safely, and to increases crops, and to sail beneficially on the water, and to cause friendship between friends and allies, and to expel flies so that they will not enter where you wish, and to destroy officials, and it is good to go into the presence of the king or other high nobles, and to cause the king and other lords to be benevolent."

So, let's analyze the election and then go onto the implementation.

This election is mixed. It has great strengths and some weaknesses. I made a judgement call that the former were much greater than the latter, but informed opinions may vary. I did not wish to wait any longer for a good talisman for this purpose.

The Moon is the principal significator in this election, and culminates. The Moon is very fast- which I believe rapidly promotes sensible manifestation and strengthens the effects overall.

The Moon is "triumphed," a term I've coined for inverse besiegement. Instead of the planet separating from an aspect with a Malefic and applying to the other, this does the same with the Benefics. In besiegement the significator is caught between a rock and a hard place; in a triumphal position, the Benefics behave like strong bodyguards which flank the traveler. The Benefics in this instance are both afflicted- yet their nature does not change and they ensure success. Beseigement remains a dire affliction even when the Malefics are weakened or fortified, and so triumphing is always among the strongest of accidental fortitudes.

Another positive factor is the Ascendant; the lord is Mercury, who receives a +2 dignification by term or bound, is fast, but is unaspected. The electional window is narrow (about six minutes) because the Ruler of the Sign the Moon is within must never be cadent and I had to wait until Mercury was eight degrees past the cusp of the 8th House boundary for this to take place. According to *Picatrix*, when the Moon's Sign Ruler is cadent, the election begins well but ends in failure.

The weaknesses of the election are that the Moon is applying to a conjunction with Mars and an opposition with Saturn after the triumphing ends, and that the Moon is in the same Sign as a Malefic (Mars.) Mars is also on an Angle; the Midheaven. These are normally very serious concerns, but I believe the role of triumphing is to shield the significator (the Moon) from afflictions. If it were the other way around and the Moon were besieged, nobody would put much weight on application to aspects of Benefics after the configuration would end.

As *Picatrix* says, there are certain configurations which can neutralize the afflictions of the Malefics, such as making them cadent and placing a Benefic on the Ascendant. I believe triumphing is another such.

Is this a perfect election? No. I'll replace it when I find a better one, but in the meanwhile I think the two talismans I made are safe and strong.

Two large quartz crystal cabochons were selected. They are inexpensive and easy to replace when a better election comes along. Both will be carried in a velvet bag to reduce scratching and impacts.

The main feature of the image is what the talisman is supposed to fortunate; a car. Before the headlights is the sigil of Venus and behind it is the sigil of Jupiter. Moon, the cosignificator, is tightly applying to a benevolent aspect of Venus and separating from a benevolent aspect Jupiter. Above the car is the sigil of the Moon and below it is the number 7, signifying the Lunar Mansion. Across the body of the car is the name of the Ruler of the 7th Mansion, SIELY. On the back is an X, which *Picatrix* advises using when one is uncertain about the image of a particular spirit for a talisman. The suffumigation was aloeswood, in very small amounts.

The image below is in different colors for clarity; they were all actually engraved with a diamond tipped stylus and not colorized. I use that here only for readability.

I am mostly including this election here, beyond as a record of my work, but as an example of how to implement the "foundational" Mansion elections with components of the Plinian/Ibn Hatim material to fill in the gaps.

The Talismans of the Inescapable Prison

Fast Moon culminating in the 25th Mansion perfecting a trine with the Greater Benefic, with a dignified and unafflicted Ascendant Ruler

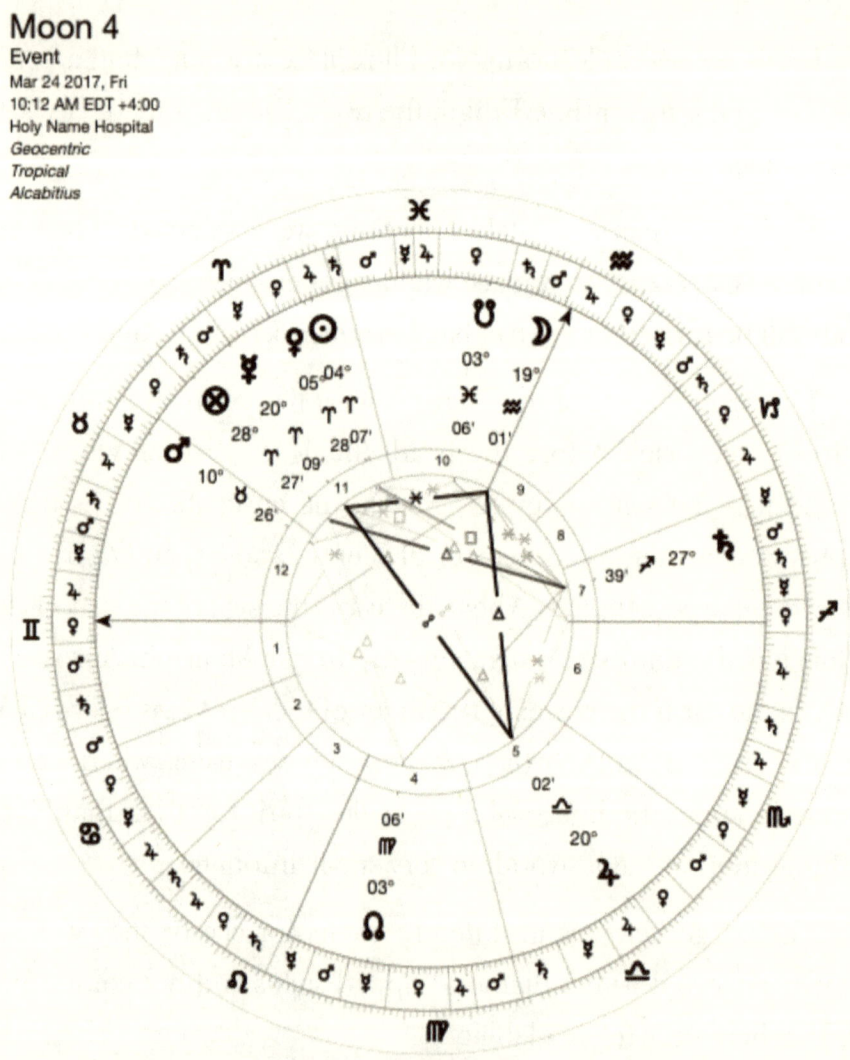

The 25th Mansion generally is for the protection of orchards and crops as per the Plinian Mansion section of *Picatrix*, but the

"Foundational Mansions" early section in the same gives a number of other options for people with brown thumbs like myself.

"In this Mansion make images to besiege cities and villages, to take enemies captive and do as much evil to them as you please, to make messengers convey their messages and quickly return, to separate wives from their husbands, to destroy harvests, to bind a man and wife or a woman and her husband so that they cannot copulate, to bind whichever part of the human body you wish so that it is not able to function, to strengthen the prison of captives; and it is good to secure buildings."

Of course, the majority of these options are for curse talismans, and would require a completely different sort of election.

But this raises a different question: clearly the hastening of messengers and the securing of buildings are benevolent and require benefic electional configurations, but what about the strengthening the prison of captives? And what is it with so many of the listings in this section either for the securing of captives or the liberation of prisoners? It's really conspicuous when you look at them as a whole.

The most obvious possibility is that magicians were often in danger of imprisonment in antiquity, and having a memorized list of potential talismans for escape was a priority. Another is that magicians were often in the employ of nobles who had a strong interest in securing enemies and rivals in their personal dungeons to fortify their positions. However, I don't think this explains it all.

Usually **SIM** texts are painfully literal at times regarding the function of talismanic recipes, but I suspect this may be an exception; I think it is also for strengthening the binding of spirits. The reason I believe this is that *Picatrix* does make references to spirit binding throughout the text suggesting that the method is quite important but is curiously evasive about specifics. To me that suggests the methods appear in coded language elsewhere in the text, and this is one of my favorite speculations–that the references to prisons and prisoners are applicable equally to human beings, spirits, and even perhaps animals.

In any case, that's all speculation for now.

The next quandary is whether strengthening a prison is benevolent or malevolent?

My take is that it is benevolent, considering that the alternative is a jailbreak. Breaking out of a prison is a form of destruction, albeit a desirable one from the subjective viewpoint of the prisoner. This is especially clear in this case when Jupiter is prominent in the electional configuration, whose attributes prioritize the augmentation and strengthening of things. Strengthening a prison is similar to the securing of buildings which is another electional option, which is unambiguously benevolent.

This election was specifically for the strengthening the prison of captives, which is especially suitable considering that the 25th Mansion's name translates (according to some) as "the star of the dungeons."

I should note that this election does not bind or imprison; it only fortifies bindings and imprisonments which already are in place.

The Moon was quite fast, applying a perfected trine to Jupiter. However, it was also applying a sextile to Mercury which is the dignified and unafflicted Ascendant Ruler, therefore reinforcing the significators. The Moon is also applying a somewhat loose sextile to Saturn which is the ruler of the Moon's Sign and a very strong consideration for success according to *Picatrix* electional rules—even though it is a Malefic.

There are possible negatives. The Ascendant Ruler is applying a trine to Saturn, which by *Picatrix* rules would weaken it. However, Mercury and Saturn have a natural amity and the trine should soften any weakening. Saturn is in a malefic Face and is in the 7th House but not on the Descendant, so I think that's acceptable. The malevolence of Saturn might make the imprisonment particularly harsh, or it may not factor in in any way. A counterindication is the role of Jupiter, which may make the imprisonment pleasant. And while Jupiter is retrograde, I do not believe this has any pertinence to the election since the planet is in a supportive role rather than being a principal player.

Six quartz crystal cabochons were made into talismans. The suffumigation was gum mastic.

The top of the cabochon was inscribed with a crescent Moon, and below it a chain with five or seven links depending upon the size of the gem. Below it were three words: STRENGTHEN, CAPTIVES, PRISONS; each below the last. On the back was inscribed an X for ease of the Mansion spirit's entry.

Normally I would have inscribed the name of the Mansion Ruler, but tarot advised against it. Perhaps the Ruler uses a different name for orchards and imprisonments.

The Rings of Memory

Fast Moon in Domicile culminating, applying to both Benefics with fortunated Ascendant Benefic Ruler and Benefic in the 1st House

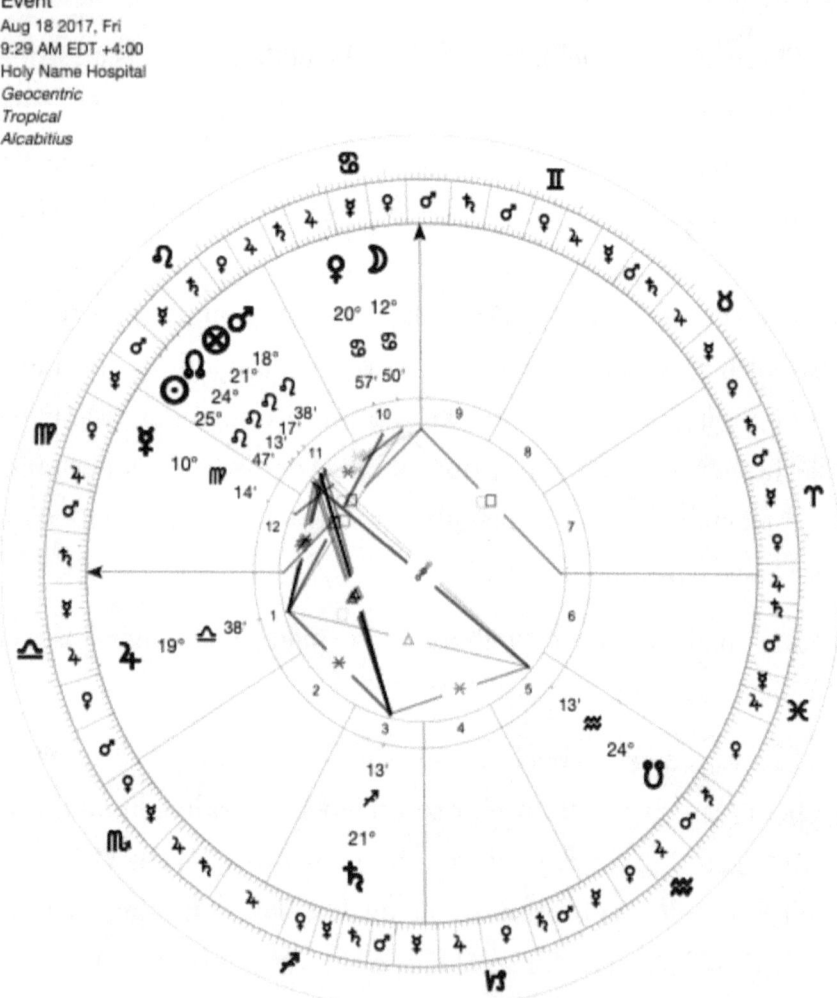

Scholastic Image Magic arose in medieval monasteries, but reached its greatest popularity among medieval and Renaissance physicians, according to contemporary research. It should be little

surprise that a great deal of priority was placed on medicinal talismans as well as those which benefit study.

This is a talisman I've wanted to make for quite a while; it's one of several configurations to enhance memory. As someone who optimally burns through about five hundred pages per day, it does me little good if I can't recall it. Furthermore, I'm just about done wasting hours looking for that missing pen or sock or passage in Cervantes.

Picatrix Book II:10: "If, under the influence of the Moon, you make this sign in the hour of the Moon, with the Moon rising, in emerald, with this stone make a seal in incense and give it to a man for good memory, and to retain knowledge."

Moon talismans:

- Improve memory, and in some configurations cause forgetfulness. The waxing and waning of the Moon signifies the transitory nature of memory. Other planets co-rule memory to a lesser degree, but it is primarily an attribute of the Moon. (One would be mistaken to assume waxing is always the retention of memory and waning is its loss, however.)

- Cure the illnesses of infants, and sometimes older children. A very useful talisman if you're a parent or a physician, but I'm neither so this is of limited interest to me.

- Increase alertness and endurance, especially while traveling. The Moon signifies speed because it is the most rapid planet; it also signifies journeys. Before modernity, a Moon talisman would be used by a traveler to walk many miles without ever becoming tired. It would also be valuable for students who want to immerse themselves in lore deep into the night without forgetfulness.

- Impart influence over mobs and riots, to gather and disperse them. The group consciousness of rioters is well known to be associated with the Moon; a social lunacy.

- Improve likeability and influence over others, especially when the Moon is very essentially dignified. The Moon is always the cosignificator of the Self, and by adding essential dignity to any significator one gains influence, authority, and trust.

It's very hard to find standard Lunar talisman elections because the rapidity of the Moon gives only one real chance daily for any configuration. Furthermore, *Picatrix* seems to indicate that the Moon should not be configured on the Ascendant, leaving only the Midheaven as the only reasonable alternative.

The difficulty of finding a valid Lunar election is why I was willing to produce these four rings during an extremely narrow eight minute electional window when the Moon was between 8 and 6 degrees of the Midheaven, never quite breaking into the 5 degrees that Ptolemy mentions before the arrival of Saturn Hour. I've already noticed its effects, so I know it's working.

As noted before, the Moon was making loose aspects to the Benefics, the Ascendant Ruler was essentially dignified, and a benefic was in the 1st House. I particularly liked the high speed of the Moon, which I've come to believe is more impactful than Lunar phase in most instances. I believe this will contribute to the strength of the memory enhancement.

Four talismanic rings were ensouled, for the time window was short. The gemstones were emerald as required, and the band was silver—the metal of the Moon. I consulted with tarot for advice on the herb matrix under the gemstone and the suffumigation. The herb beneath the ring was black poppy seed—a Lunar herb—which has associations with the mind and mental states. The suffumigation was amber, which I believe signified the preservation of memory, like an insect preserved in amber.

Rather than use the primary talismans to create secondary talismans out of incense, as the instructions suggest, my goal was simply to make rings. This is partially because I was not casting in silver to make a negative talismanic mold for the incense, and because that seems to me a project best saved for when the Moon is within five degrees of the Midheaven. I may choose to make memory incense with these, but that is not my intention now.

There are many unusual talismanic recipes in *Picatrix* and other canonical texts of SIM. Some may puzzle you, but rather than dismiss them as aberrations I believe they have much to teach us about the nature of the spiritual universe. They also frequently have powers which you may think are irrelevant to your needs today, but will reveal their value tomorrow.

That's advice you'll definitely benefit from remembering.

The Rings of the Fortunate Mystic

Fortunated Moon applying to conjoin Alcyone culminating with the North Node Ascending in Perfection

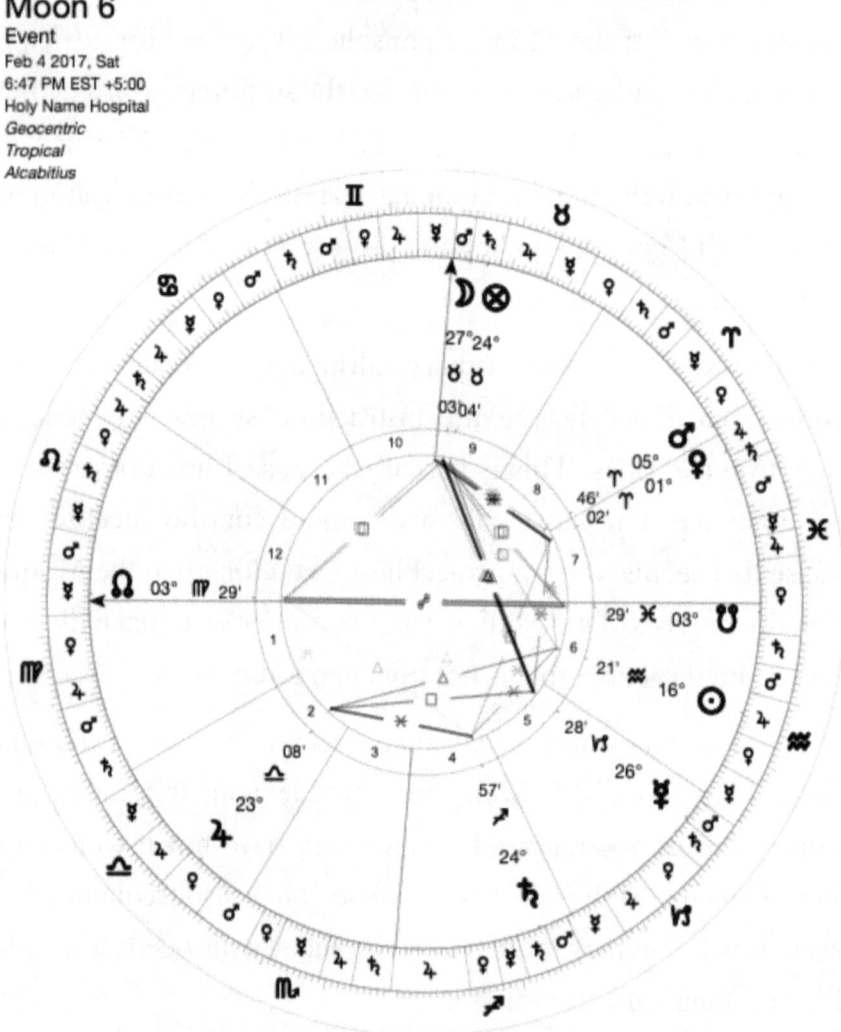

I'd long ago nearly given up on finding a good Pleiades talismanic election, but stumbled across this one so close to the date that I'm glad that I'd ordered a few quartz crystal rings for

another project recently or I'd have missed a treasure! This one was quite worth waiting for.

Alcyone culminates, the Moon is very fast and she applies to a fortunate aspect of a benefic, albeit out-of-Sign. The Ascendant Ruler is fast and likewise applying to a benefic. The aspect is sextile, which is closely connected to Venus, the benefic in question. The Moon is separating from a conjunction with Algol, but I think that's safe. Finally, and most excellently, the North Node is exactly on the Ascendant.

Now, the most extensive instructions on how to create a Pleiades talisman comes from the *Quindecim Stellis,* but there are similar details in Agrippa and in the *Confessio Amantis.*

"Fennel seed with frankincense and quicksilver placed under a crystal with the appropriate character [engraved on it], with the Moon conjunct the Pleiades rising or at midheaven, preserves the eyesight, summons demons and the spirits of the dead, calls the winds, and reveals secrets and things that are lost."

The left sigil is from the *Quindecim Stellis* text and the right is from Agrippa. I tend to use the more complex *Quindecim Stellis* versions unless pressed for time. Most people seem to think the Agrippa sigils are degenerate and certainly date more recently.

Above the sigil I engraved the name of the angel of the Pleiades from the Greek Magical Papyri, ZIZAUBIO, and below it I engraved the common sigil of the North Node of the Moon.

Now, the big problem with Pleiades talismans is that quicksilver is a deadly poison. Tarot divination has led me to believe that a passable substitute for this talisman are poppy seeds, perhaps because of the fever dreams opium can produce. It works well enough as far as I can tell.

Four snow quartz cabochon gemstones set in sterling silver wire rings were used. I mixed the poppy seeds with glue along with fennel seeds and frankincense grains below the gemstones towards the end of the electional window. The suffumigation was predominately frankincense but fennel and poppy were included as well. No scented oils were used this time.

The Talismans of Awestruck Dread

11th Lunar Mansion with Mars

Moon 7
Event
Mar 2 2015, Mon
9:58 PM EST +5:00
Holy Name Hospital
Geocentric
Tropical
Alcabitius

This is one of those experimental elections which either curse the living shit out of me or work fabulously. Somebody needs to test this stuff out, might as well be me. Kids, don't try this at home!

The Moon is slow, too slow to normally create a talisman but is held aloft by the benefics which flank it; to the rear by Venus, while before it rallies a bodily conjoined Jupiter- retrograde but dignified. The Moon also is opposing Mercury, but is surely protected by the benefics. Yet a conjunction with a retrograde planet is indeed a consideration which makes this an experimental election. Is the power of being protected by the benefics enough to overcome an application to a retrograde planet albeit the most benevolent one? I suspect yes.

Yet the true controversy of this election is the Ascendant. It is governed by Mars in domicile, but Mars is conjoined with the South Node. And here is the grand design; some sources believe that a malefic with the Dragon's Tail is dangerous and others claim it is greatly fortunated thereby. This is the true experiment at the heart of this election. If it is a dud, then that can be explained by the Moon; but if it is destructive that can only mean a malefic with the S.N. is woeful.

All things considered, if it works well it will be because this Lunar Mansion is compatible with the attributes of Mars as cosignifcator. This is a talisman to instill fear and respect from those beneath you, while eliciting favor from those in positions of power.

Picatrix Rubeus pages 288-289, the Plinian Mansions: "The eleventh Mansion is Azobra, and it is that you will be feared and receive good things. When the Moon is in this Mansion, make in a table of gold the image of a man riding a lion, holding a lance in his right hand and holding the ear of the lion with his left hand, and in front of this figure write the name of the lord of this Mansion. Say: "You, Necol, bring glory to me that I shall be feared by men, and so that their fear shall cause them to tremble when they behold me; and quiet the heart of the king and of lords and of men of high estate that they may grant me honors and dignities." Carry this tablet with you, and it shall be as you have requested. Know that Necol is the name of the lord of this Mansion."

No suffumigation was given in the *Picatrix* text, but Ibn Hatim (in his *De Imaginibus*) offers lion's hair. This is less helpful than it might have been around 800AD. (Anybody know a zookeeper or a veterinarian with a really big electric shaver?) After consultation with tarot, this was substituted with the hair of a black cat and storax (from Alchemy Works.)

Three quartz cabochons were selected with NECOL above the described figure, and placed in a yellow flannel bag along with chunks of gum mastic. I didn't have gold handy, but this should work nicely. Or so says tarot.

The thing is that a malefic dignified allows it to resist its more dangerous attributes in the same way a conjunction with the South Node ought to. Unless the opposite opinion is valid.

My hope of course is that this will make the ASC super duper dignified Essentially and Accidentally. And make me a loved and feared prince, just like Niccolo Machiavelli actually preferred.

Defixios of Burning Hatred

Moon in 5th Mansion, combust, besieged, Cancer ascending

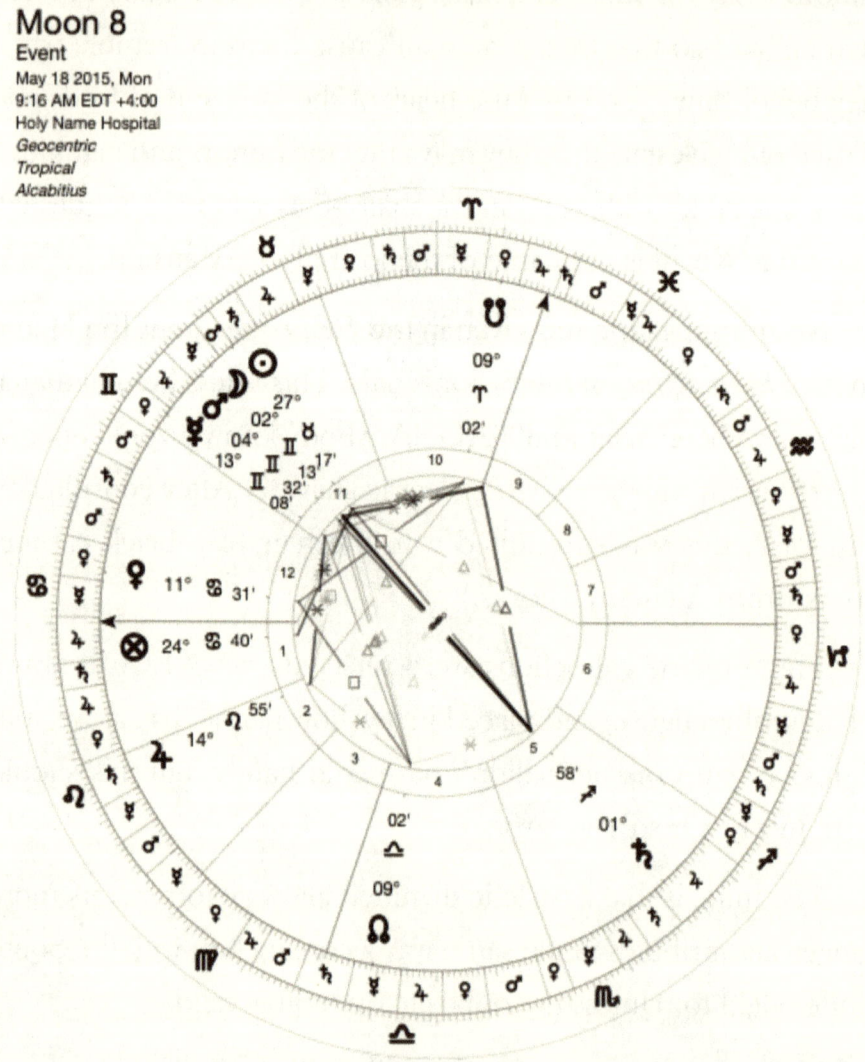

Fifth Mansion effects include "to destroy the friendship between two people" in *Picatrix*, when the principal planets are afflicted. Some contend that combustion and/or besiegement are limited by Sign boundaries; I disagree. This election has both, a fairly toxic combo. Cancer is also a Sign associated with curses in Traditional magical texts, including *Picatrix* if I recall properly. The Moon is succeedent, but in the 11th House where she can do the damage intended. She is fast, thus indicating rapid and palpable effects.

Nine lead disks were used, as mini-defixios to be planted on the person or property of targets. The sigil of the Moon was placed above an X, which *Picatrix* advises to use when the character or image of a spirit are not known. Storax was used as a suffumigation.

Lead would not normally be an appropriate choice for a Lunar talisman, but the silvery dullness of lead is suitable for curses depending on the power of the Moon.

The Rings of Fortunate Meetings
Eighth Mansion for Friendship, Love, and the Society of Travelers

Moon 9
Event
Aug 13 2013, Tue
9:20 AM EDT +4:00
Holy Name Hospital
Geocentric
Tropical
Alcabitius

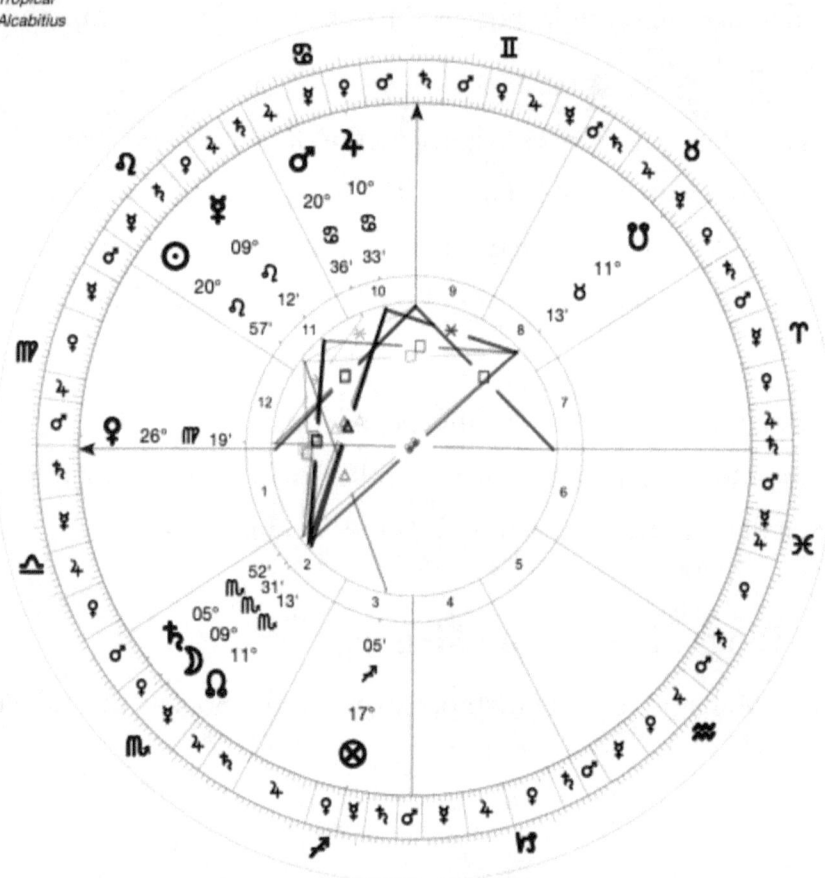

This was a somewhat experimental election, with the Moon unusually slow but with mitigating factors. The Moon culminated while applying to Jupiter in exaltation while Venus in domicile ascended. Having a benefic on Asc or MC rectifies an afflicted Moon, so this doubles up on that consideration.

Being that this was a highly benevolent configuration, I chose to use the *Abraham the Jew* variant design on quartz cabochons in silver, displaying two children holding hands with the name of the Mansion Ruler inscribed across the middle. The "herb" beneath the ring was sulfur, as per the Plianian Mansion instructions but the suffumigation was frankincense and myrrh as per the Hockley *AtJ* text. The *AtJ* material in this instance is compatible and surely derived from the alternative Mansion section in *Picatrix*; it is only the image and suffumigation which are specific and novel.

The Moon applying to conjoin a highly dignified Jupiter was quite suggestive of friendship, and so I believe this was a very strong project.

The Oil used (based on divination, which is why it is so odd) was Aunt Sally's Lucky Dream Oil.

The Talismans of Friendship and Love

Very fast Moon culminating in the Sixth Mansion, triumphed Ascendant Ruler, North Node loosely on the Ascendant

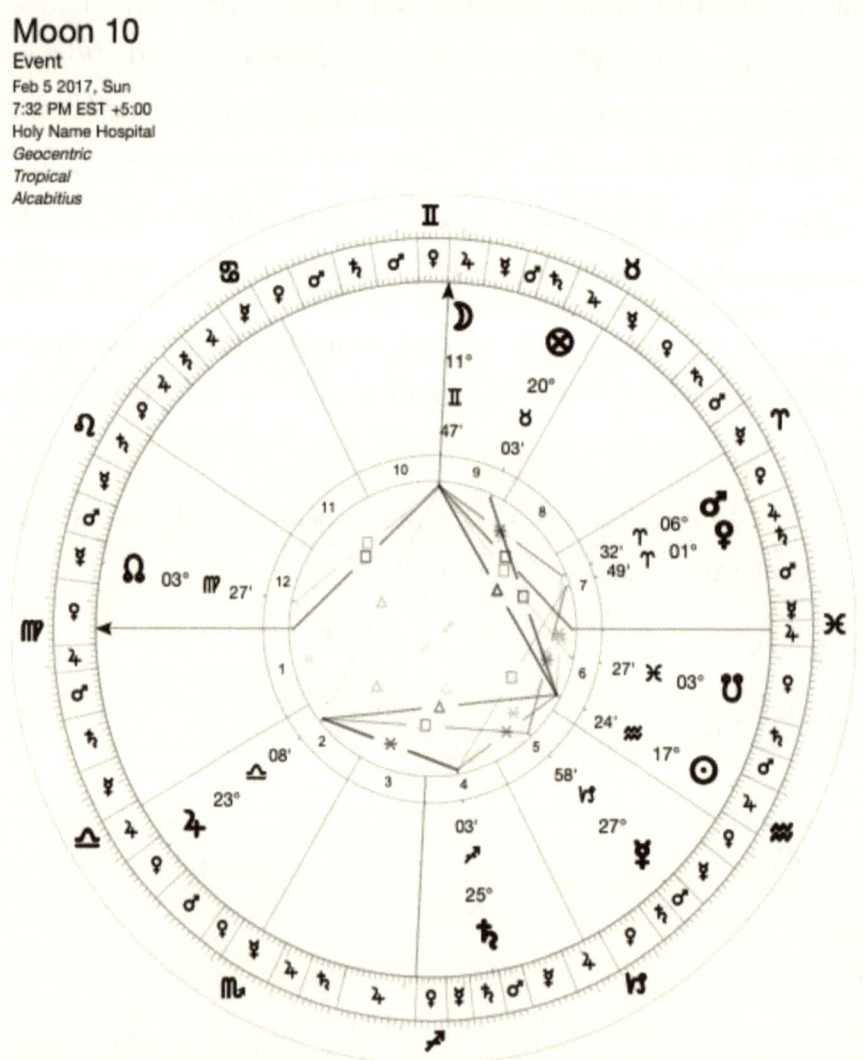

Here we have a very fast Moon culminating in the Sixth Mansion, the North Node somewhat distant from the Ascendant but probably providing some increased strength towards the

beginning of the election, the Moon making a fortunate aspect to the Sun (a neutral planet), but the Ascendant Ruler (Mercury) in the very fortunate Fifth House and triumphed (AKA reverse/benevolent besiegement) by separating from Jupiter and applying to Venus. All quite good.

The primary usage of the Sixth Mansion talisman by way of in the Plinian Mansion section of *Picatrix* (in turn derived from Ibm Hatim) is for love. However talismans for friendship are also options, as well as talismans for hunting and a variety of destructive options.

"The sixth mansion is called Athaya. It is from 4 degrees 17 minutes and 10 seconds of Gemini all the way to 17 degrees 8 minutes and 36 seconds of the same sign. In this Mansion make images for the destruction of cities and villages, and to besiege them with armies, and for the enemies of kings to exact vengeance, and to destroy crops and trees, and to cause friendship between two people, to improve hunting in the country, and to destroy medicines so that when they are taken they do not work."

That's from *Picatrix* III:4, and talismans for destruction are only used when the Ascendant and Moon are afflicted here, which is not the case.

"The sixth Mansion is Achaya and it is for putting love between two people. When the Moon is passing through this Mansion, make two images from white wax, make them embrace each other, and wrap them in white silk. Suffumigate them with amber and lignum aloes, and say: 'You, Nedeyrahe, bring together so and so and so and so, and place between them friendship and love.' It will be as you wish. Know that Nedeyrahe is the name of the lord of this Mansion."

That's from the pseudo-Plinian section of *Picatrix* in *Picatrix* IV:9.

"The image is two persons embracing. You should shape them from white wax, and you should fumigate it with camphor and damp aloes-wood. The name of its lord is Anari. Wrap it in a shining rag, hold it with you, and beseech it. You will be brought to love and to medical treatment. The name(s) of its stars are al-Zara and al-Mizan."

That's from Ibn Hatim. (No, I'm not sure what the medical treatment thing is about.)

How did I arrange this? I took four quartz crystal cabochons–which is the best substitute for white wax talismans that you want to last–and engraved the image of embracing friends on some and embracing lovers on others. I engraved ANARI across the middle of the cabochon and the names of the targets (when appropriate) on the flat back of the gemstones. I then wrapped each gemstone in a little packet of white silk along with a calligraphic printout of the names for extra emphasis.

For suffumigation I used Baltic amber (since it's pretty cheap) and some very nice lignum aloes (AKA aloeswood) which is not cheap at all. In retrospect, camphor in place of amber would have worked, but is more sexual and that's not what I was necessarily aiming for here. Amber is nice enough.

Talisman of Desire: Alahue

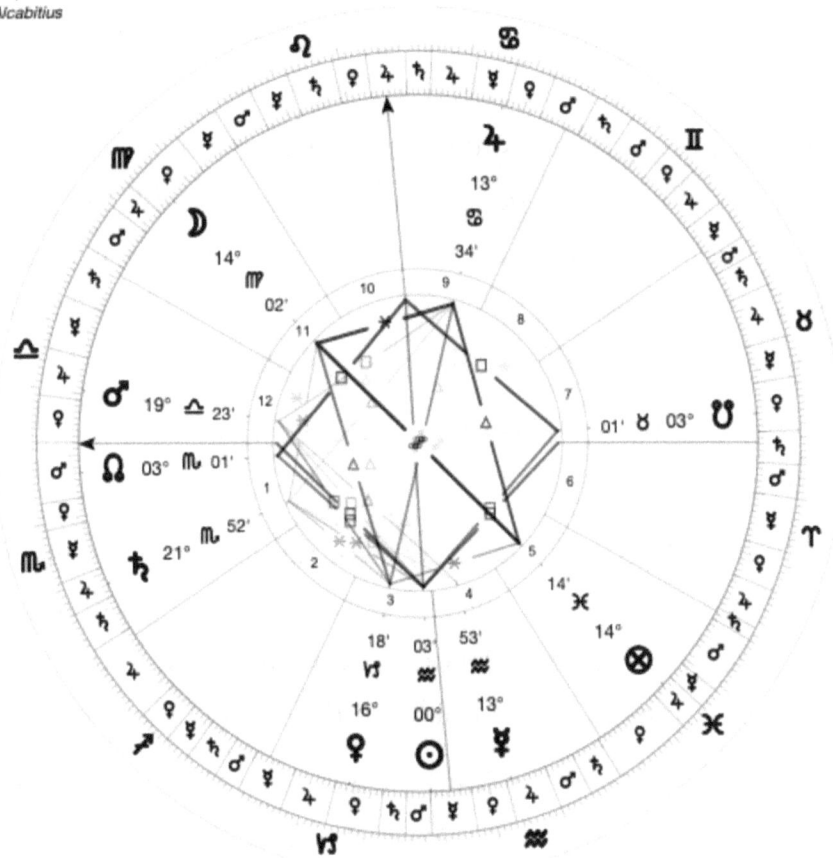

This was somewhat experimental, but worth noting.

"The thirteenth Mansion is Alahue, and it is for the liberation of men who are not able to come to women and for putting love between men and women. When the Moon is passing through this Mansion, fashion from red wax the image of an erect man (that is, with an erect penis); and let it be in all ways the image of a man desiring to couple with a woman. From white wax fashion the image of a woman. Bind the two images together face to face, and suffumigate them with amber and lignum aloes, and wrap them in a piece of white silk which has been washed in rosewater; and on either image write the name of the one you desire. If a woman shall carry these images with her, she will be most strongly desired by the man whose name is upon the image - which is to say, when he sees her. If another is tied or bound, who is not able to perform with women, if he shall carry the images with him it shall be dissolved and he will be able to perform with women. Know that the name of the lord of this Mansion is Azerut."

That being the Plinian version. The more general *Picatrix* commentary is:

"In this Mansion make images for the increase of trade and profit, the increase of harvests, for travelers to have good journeys on the roads, for the completion of buildings, for the freedom of captives, and the binding of nobles to have good from them."

In any case, I put the Moon in the 11th House this time in order to take advantage of the North Node on the Ascendant. But the great strength of this election is that the Moon is between benevolent aspects with the benefics! The Moon's aspect to Saturn is a problem, but the Moon is waning, the aspect is benevolent, and the Moon between the benefics is a fortitude which easily surpasses that concern.

I created two loose stone talismans; two lapis lazuli cabochons, one for me and one for an unspecified recipient. (The one for me is not for virility, ahem.) Lapis lazuli is the primary stone of the Moon, and this should suffice even though the image is of an embracing couple on one object. AZERUT was inscribed across the middle. The suffumigation was amber and aloeswood. No oil was used, but both will be sewn into bags of white silk and anointed with rosewater.

Often questions are raised regarding love magic and consent.

I'm not sure I'd do it for myself, but I might be more flexible with a client. I'm a die-hard romantic, but not everybody is- and after watching the Jerry Springer Show a few times have decided that many people don't know what's best for themselves, in love or just about anything else either.

A better answer is that just as we evolve from a Disney version of magic to a *Picatrix* version of magic, we are wise to do the equivalent with love. Real magic is not as easy as the wave of a wand nor real love predestined and effortless- though one can make either seem to be the case with some untold effort. Yet that does not remove the marvel that is the process of magic, nor make love any less worth living for. It simply replaces a child's wonder with an adult's pride from craftsmanship and artistry. The fact that both require brainpower and sweat make neither any less gateways to the divine world.

I don't really think there was a significant role for undirected love magic in ancient times. Back then, marriages were arranged as a rule, and that meant love magic was mostly to seduce someone's spouse.

That considered, can this sort of love magic be justified?

Well. I've tried it once or twice as an experiment and it has worked. But I did it ethically; targets who I was not overly interested in romantically, who lived far away. So I did not take advantage of the situation, but probably left the targets feeling confused and a bit rejected. At least I know it works, and works rather well.

And it does not wear off, if done right. Ever.

What I learned from it, is that when a target is affected, they are compelled to compliance, but also to pleasure. I suspect that a person under a love spell and united with their seducer is high as a kite.

There are worse fates than being blissfully enslaved to one's sweetheart, forever and ever, and never getting bored, never having doubts, never discontented...

One might argue (a little mischievously) that it's better than conventional love. Because that tends to fade, or even shatter, with the passing of years... and one has a larger share of Divine Eros in it, the cosmic love which all earthly romance is a dull shadow of...

But I'm not brave or ruthless enough to test that out.

The Gems of Bedazzling Ardor
The Talismans of the Twenty-Sixth Mansion

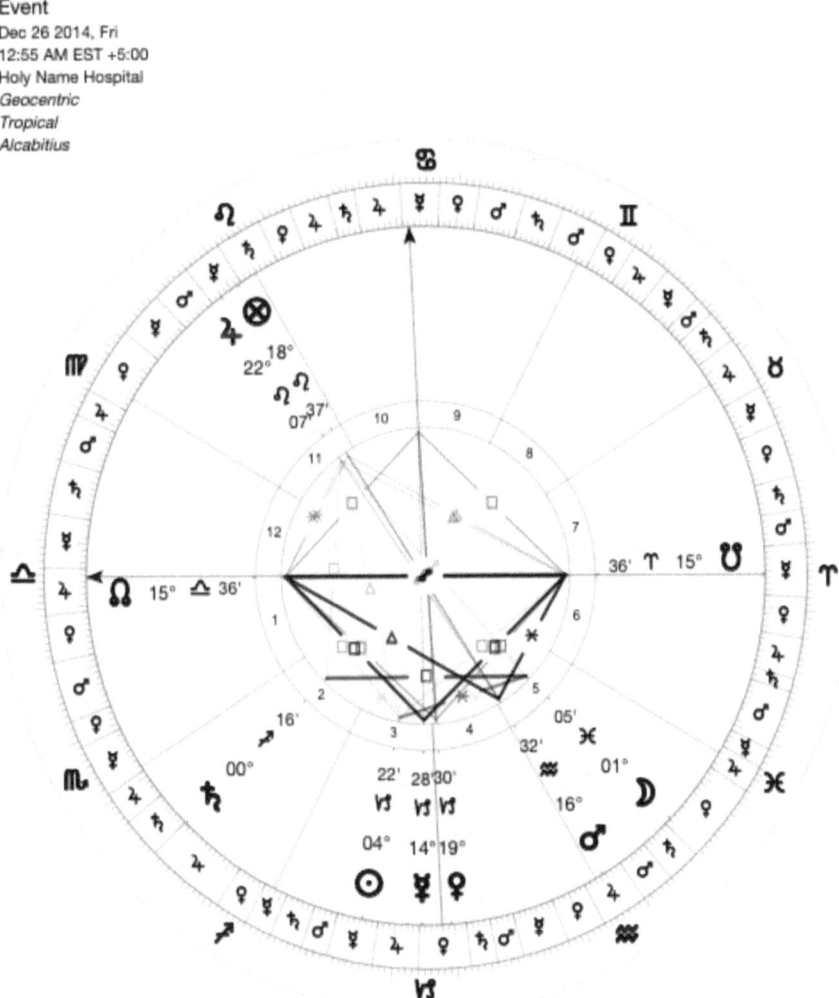

Picatrix Rubeus, page 292: "When the Moon is passing through it, take white wax and mastic and melt them together; from these fashion the image of a woman with her hair unbound and before her a vessel placed as if to receive her hair. Suffumigate it with sweet-smelling odors, and say: 'You, Tagriel, bring me to the love and friendship of such and such a woman.' Place the image in a small bag, and place with it also some of the most sweet-smelling of substances; carry it with you, and it shall be completed as you have requested. Know that Tagriel is the name of the lord of this Mansion."

Ibn Hatim via Lippincott: "The image is a woman whose hair hangs down; on her are varieties of coloured cloths; between her two hands is a pot in which is a perfume (with which) she perfumes herself. You should shape her, in accordance with the name of whomever among women you wish, out of white wax and mastic. Fumigate it with varieties of perfumes. You should write on her chest the name of the man overcoming her love for herself. You should keep the image in the house so that she refrains from going to him, if God wills. The name of her lord is Nafsiyal taghriyal. Its speciality is for love that she entice (?) the man marvellously and promote lust. It is four stars, similar to a bucket."

This was a slightly unconventional election and also slightly unconventional in implementation.

The Moon was in the 5th House of good fortune and pleasure, while the North Node was conjoined to the Ascendant. The Moon was extremely fast, waxing, and in a Sign whose ruler was not cadent (though retrograde.) The Moon was making benevolent aspects to the Sun and Mercury; the former very tightly.

These were loose gem talismans. Three lapis lazuli cabochons (fairly large) were inscribed with the image described, but with the

North Node sigil at the apex, the number 26 at the bottom, and TAGRIEL on the obverse center. The suffumigation was a blend of dried rosebuds and lignum aloes. No oil was used.

The North Node functions similarly to a benefic planet when placed on the ASC or MC, and adds strength to any election- particularly one which requires an overcoming of an obstacle or an adversary. It is dependent on the strength of the election's configuration overall, for though it magnifies the luck and power of other factors by itself it is highly unstable and cannot be the sole power drawn upon. Fortunately the speed, phase and aspects of the Moon are good enough for a potent election on their own, and though the placement of the Moon in a Succedent House easily offset by the benevolence and relevance to the election's goal. The Dragon's Head is really just the cherry on top, but what a cherry it is!

Due to the relative softness of the lapis lazuli and the intense speed of the Moon, these talismans should be very fast acting. Their durability at this stage is not clear, but the configuration suggests to me that the effect would be extensive and enduring.

The Talismans of Union

The Talismans of Nedeyrahe, Lord of the Sixth Mansion of the Moon

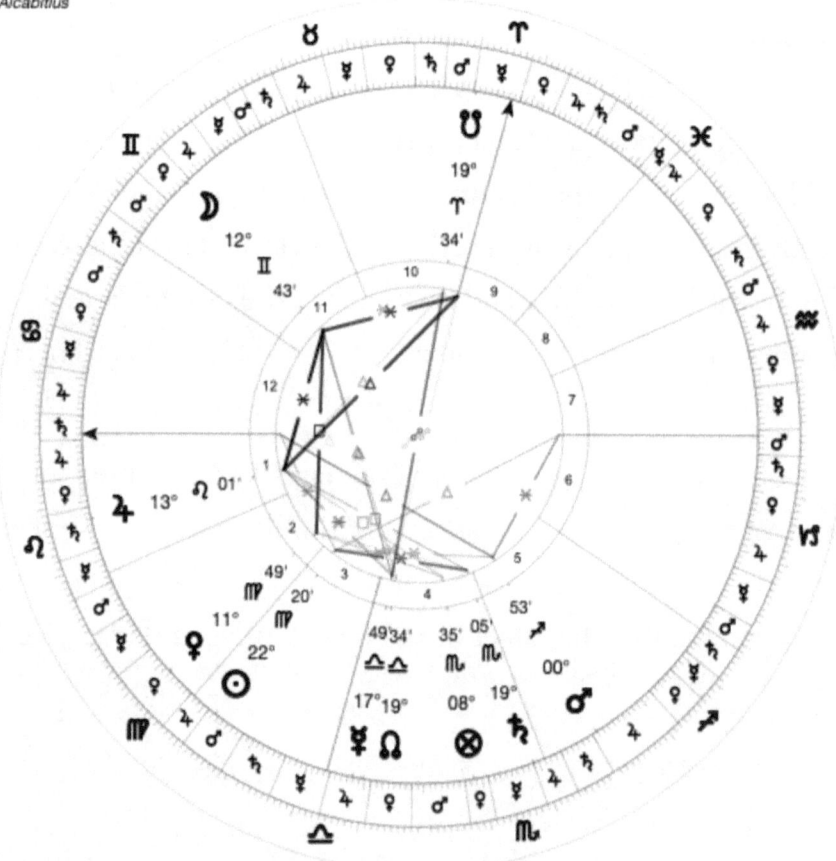

Picatrix says in the Pseudo-Pliny Mansions: "The sixth Mansion is Achaya and it is for putting love between two people. When the Moon is passing through this Mansion, make two

images from white wax, make them embrace each other, and wrap them in white silk. Suffumigate them with amber and lignum aloes, and say: 'You, Nedeyrahe, bring together so and so and so and so, and place between them friendship and love.' It will be as you wish. Know that Nedeyrahe is the name of the lord of this Mansion."

Ibn Hatim, surely the origin of this section, says much the same.

The election was rather novel, as you shall see shortly, so I took the opportunity with whatever I had at hand.

Fortunately, I keep incense-grade amber and powdered aloeswood handy, and recently bought quartz cabochons in bulk from eBay. (White wax figures seem to substitute well with quartz cabochons if clear or milky. Color matters, and in spite of the temptation to glue two cabochons together, doing this as a single gem has proven effective on prior projects.)

Now, the first thing you'll note is that the Moon is not on the MC or even angular. It is, however, in a benevolent House (although just barely succedent) and fast enough. But what makes this such a dynamic election is that the Moon is TIGHTLY flanked or Warded or Celebrated by the Benefics- something which we sometimes call reverse besiegement. That's always a good thing.

I put Cancer on the ASC even though it's at the end of the Sign simply because Warding is such a tremendously positive accidental dignity that it easily beat anything going on with the Sun when Leo was to Ascend.

I also wanted to get Jupiter in the 1st House, because that would strengthen the election by the mere virtue of having a Benefic there.

It also is good that the Moon was trining a dignified Mercury (itself tightly conjoining the North Node) and the North Node as well. It is an additional fortitude that the Moon is the House of Mercury (Gemini) while trining Mercury.

The result was a five minute electional window and two talismans. (I'm lightning at 2am if you give me some Red Bull.)

I have a roll of white silk which I cut out a pair of rough disks and glued the cabochon within, along with a bit of the amber and a pinch of the aloeswood. The inscription was of a man and a woman intertwined naked, with the text "Nedeyrahe, join XY and XX" on it, with the names substituted.

The main innovation of this experiment was that I combined the Plinian instructions with the incantations on page 50 of the *Rubeus* edition.

"You, Nedeyrahe, let XY be joined to XX and conjoined with her, as fire, air, and water with earth; and let him so be moved toward her as the rays of the Sun move the light of Earth and its virtues; and let they and their works be coupled together in their vision as heaven is conjoined with its stars, and trees with their flowers. Let his spirit be thus raised on high and sublime above the spirit of **XX**, as the water is raised up over the earth; and let each of the aforesaid be unable to eat, or drink, or dance, or take pleasure in anything without the other."

Recited three times, in part because Nedeyrahe is not easy to say at 2AM.

Chapter Seven

Other Stellar Talismans

Aries Medical Talismans

Other 01
Event
Mar 25 2018, Sun
6:56 AM EDT +4:00
Holy Name Hospital
Geocentric
Tropical
Alcabitius

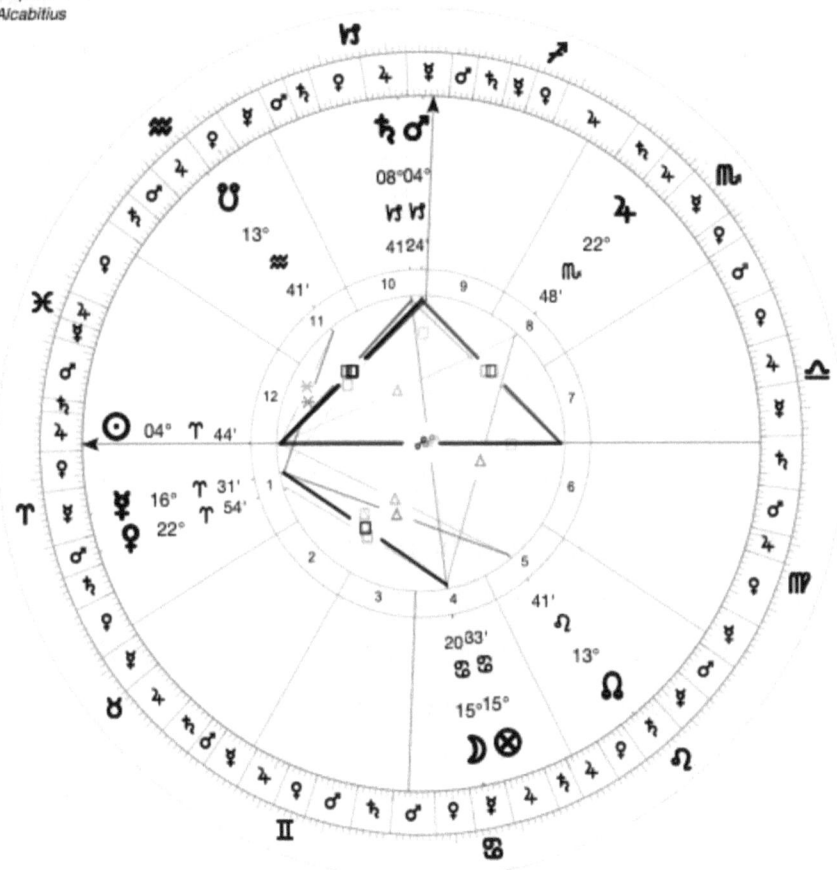

Sun in Aries Talismans for Healing the Infirmities of the Head

Contemporary research into the distribution of texts on magic in medieval and Renaissance England suggests that theurgical and necromantic texts were concentrated in monasteries, but texts on Scholastic Image Magic were concentrated in the libraries of physicians. This does appear to indicate that physicians had a particular interest in astral magic and probably were also one of the few occupations which would have had the necessary background in astrology to make use of it. A survey of the breadth of the canonical literature of Scholastic Image Magic does suggest a preponderance of formulas for talismans which were used medicinally. While theurgical and necromantic rituals for longevity, relief of ailments, prevention and cures do exist, going back as far as the Testament of Solomon and ancient Mesopotamia, the additional emphasis is notable in SIM.

Part of this is simply that the boundary between medicine and magic has been quite blurry up until relatively recently in history, and both traditional medicine and Scholastic Image Magic have had an astrological basis. We may speculate, however, that astrological talismans may have had a special efficacy in an era not otherwise known for medical advancement.

This has been a significant interest of mine: the use of magic to prevent, treat and cure diseases, and extend animal and human longevity. The greatest successes in my experiments have been relatively recent, and involve Scholastic Image Magic talismans applied directly to patients or a variety of medicinal substances exposed to their proximity become secondary talismans and are then brought to the patient and ingested or otherwise applied.

In all cases I must note that these treatments were in the form of complementary therapies. I am not a physician and do not pretend to be one, traditional or modern. At no point during my experiments have I or would I ask a patient to alter their treatment from whatever their doctors require. Nevertheless, I do think that talismanic remedies have very special merits and are quite deserving of revival and extensive research.

Though many of these cases deserve their own separate blog post, I have used talismans to help patients with a variety of conditions which include metastatic brain cancer, ovarian cancer, stomach cancer, heart disease, strokes, diabetes, COPD (chronic obstructive pulmonary disease), c. diff (clostridium difficile) infections, erectile dysfunction, fevers, migraine headaches, and even the common cold. In every instance the talismans seemed to improve outcomes; often quite dramatically. As someone who once was studying to become an M.D., I understand how bold these claims sound and I stand behind them.

The prevention of disease and resisting the aging process is a less glamorous side to this system of magic, but I wear talismans for these purposes at all times. When you are young and healthy, talismans which procure love and wealth and vengeance and knowledge and power are the most seductive. When your body doesn't quite work the way it used to, those priorities shift very quickly. As a former caregiver that is comfortably in his middle age, the use of magic to improve vitality and extend life has been a front burner project for about a decade, and things grow more interesting and promising every year.

Another reason why medical magic fascinates me is that it is results-oriented and in many instances easy to validate. If a technique has a statistically significant rate of improving outcomes in diseases which are hard or impossible to treat, it is one step forward in making the case that magic is not quackery or delusion, but objectively real and of immense value.

When I first immersed myself in the study of astrological talismans I was surprised by an unusual omission. Talismans of many sorts for the seven planets had their own recipes; over 70 for the Decans or Faces, well over 100 options for the Lunar Mansions, and many other varieties. But there was no mention of talismans which corresponded to the twelve Zodiacal Signs. I bitterly concluded that this was not accidental; that the Signs themselves had no power unique to them except when combined with a planet or point which activated it. That the Signs were simply too passive in their cosmic function to create viable talismans with unique properties. I was disappointed, but reconciled myself to this interpretation.

When John Michael Greer and Christopher Warnock translated the *Picatrix* and I began studying it, I finally came across Zodiacal talismans. They weren't anything I was expecting, however. They were a series of medical talismans, which were designed to repair illnesses which affected different parts of the body: internal and external, by the somewhat shaky medieval understanding of medicine and anatomy. They were generally dependent on the position of the Sun as it passed through the Zodiac, but were otherwise profoundly complex electional recipes. Even more frustrating, most of them seemed to require being made of gold; a metal whose price was fairly high. Their application, however, was simple. One bound the talisman to the appropriate body part and the patient experienced immediate relief. Over an unspecified amount of time, they promised a permanent cure.

During the following years I made various attempts to secure affordable gold plates or foil upon which I could make the more expensive Zodiacal talismans to no avail. My eventual goal was to have a set of all twelve so I could treat the broadest possible range of ailments, but this project was postponed until I could obtain the materials. Every so often I would go back and skim the chapter on Zodiacal talismans, and eventually I made a small discovery.

While it was particularly difficult to distinguish the internal organs cited in *Picatrix* and their relation to modern understandings of anatomy, external features were far clearer. One which caught my eye was the Aries talisman to heal all infirmities of the head. Not only did this promise help for a wide variety of difficult to treat illnesses in modern medicine, but the recipe did not require pure gold but an alloy of gold and silver that would be far more affordable.

The lure and the problem with *Picatrix*'s assignment of infirmities of the head is that it's not immediately obvious which diseases it would actually treat. In the medieval medical model, major clinical depression would be melancholia; a personality type resulting from an excess of black bile in the upper intestines, thus not in the brain at all. Many other diseases that today we identify as neurological would have been assigned to the blood, the liver, or the heart. A stroke which paralyzed a limb would be governed by the Zodiacal Sign of the limb and thus require a different talisman altogether.

Nevertheless, other types of strokes, brain tumors, concussions, migraines, dementia, probably epilepsy and the manic portion of bipolar disorder seem good candidates for being identified with the brain in the medieval model, and treatable using an Aries talisman. Many of these are diseases which are hard to treat, and in some cases quite terrifying.

As soon as I realized that this sort of talisman would be highly valuable and fascinating to create, I began looking for upcoming elections. As I will discuss shortly, the conditions for the election are very uncommon and difficult, but a viable electional window was evident less than a week from the search.

I then went on a frantic mission to find gold-silver alloy disks. I found gold-plated silver disks and ordered them, but they were delayed in transit and arrived a week late. As a backup I ordered several other types of gold disks for engraving, and just in the nick of time a selection of ten gold-plated bronze disks arrived. The materials were imperfect, and the size was much smaller than the formula seemed to require; yet there was no time to obtain better.

Initial experiments with these gold-plated Aries talismans are highly promising, and I am looking for volunteers in the vicinity of the New York City area with relevant ailments to validate their efficacy.

"Hermes Trismegistus explains in his book On Images how to calculate images for each and every part of the human body and under which face of the signs to make them. Take pure gold and make a seal and write on it the image of a lion... Bind the seal around the loins or kidneys. I have tested this, and found that one who does this will not suffer thereafter... This happens likewise for the sufferings of the other members of the body, according to their manner and form, and the appropriate symbolism of the planets...

"Aries. This figure is a ram with no tongue. Its properties are for all the infirmities of the head. While it may be made when the Sun is in the first or third or fifth degree of Aries, this figure will be of no benefit unless it is made when the Moon is waxing or full. These are the conditions of the figure. Saturn and Mars must be direct, Jupiter is not in Aquarius and Venus is not in Virgo, which is the sign of her fall, and Mercury is not in Taurus; make the figure between the first degree of Aries and the fifth degree of the first face, and do not make it in the second face (they have said elsewhere that the second face pertains to the eyes and the third to the ears, whence you must pay attention to the degrees), and when the Sun and Jupiter are completely above the earth; and make it in the hour of the Sun. Others say that it is good in the day and hour of Jupiter. And make it from gold and silver to the weight of 7 grains of common wheat. This is proven." *-Picatrix* II:12

The Sun is only in those degrees three days a year. Requiring that the Moon be waxing or full cuts the opportunities roughly in half. Having both the Sun and Jupiter above the earth is less than half of the potential elections; furthermore, Jupiter is on a twelve year cycle through the Zodiac, so one can assume at least seven consecutive years when this election is entirely impossible. Requiring the planetary hour be that of the Sun divides the opportunities into a seventh. The other conditions reduce the chances of this election further, but by smaller amounts. The result of this level of complexity is that one will usually have to wait many years for a minimally viable election.

In the election used, the Sun was Ascending in 4 Aries (the fifth degree) in the Hour and Day of the Sun. The Moon was waxing. Saturn and Mars were direct. Jupiter was Retrograde but not in Aquarius, and Venus was in Aries though not in Virgo, Mercury was Retrograde but not in Taurus and close to the Ascendant. The Sun and Jupiter were above the horizon. Though not cited as a condition, the Moon was in mixed conditions of hard and soft aspects to Benefics and neutral planets. The Moon was very fast, and Angular in the 4th House. The Moon is conjunct the Part of Fortune, albeit separating; I'm not sure how much of a factor this is.

The big problem is that the Sun is besieged by the Malefics. Nevertheless, I felt that with such challenging requirements it might be pardonable and worth a shot. Normally a significator besieged by the Malefics would be prohibitive, but so many other features of the election were positive that I felt that it would compensate. At the worst, the talisman will be less effectual or slow-acting; I do not believe the configuration capable of doing harm because the Moon is making no applying aspects to the Malefics.

There was a flurry of Solar-type talismanic elections recently, so I believe that I used cloves as a suffumigation but may need to revise that later as am no longer certain and my notes are ambiguous.

Ten talismans were made in gold-plated bronze. The image of a ram was inscribed on one side and the sigil of the Sun on the opposite. Inscribing on such a small surface was challenging but I practiced a bit and all of the rams are recognizable as such.

One has been claimed by me, and three have been sewn into Los Angeles Rams baseball caps for use by any number of patients. Aries is a ram, after all. Six remain in storage for different forms of application.

Because there might be concern about the safety of a talisman with a besieged significator I wore one of these talismans under a bandage on my head for about a month and suffered no ill effects. Conversely, it appeared to be effective for my relatively mild medical concerns.

Magic Rings of Procyon

Our primary source for the talismans of Procyon comes from the *Quindecim Stellis*, a ubiquitous British grimoire which dates back to at least the fourteenth century. Its first appearance is in an incomplete form as a chapter in John Gower's *Confessio Amantis,* an extremely popular work written between 1386 and 1390, which describes the stones, herbs, and some of the properties of fifteen prominent fixed stars collectively known as the Behenian stars or the Behenii.

John Gower's work is ostensibly for the moral education of a young king; a common genre of book in that period, but clearly directed to and received by a far wider audience. In the relevant passage, atop his tower the legendary wizard Nectanebus teaches young prince Alexander of Macedonia the nature of the heavenly bodies and the powers concealed therein. It is through the use of magic rings of this nature that medieval readers were informed through this and many other texts that Alexander the Great conquered the world. Though largely forgotten today, Gower was a contemporary and rival of Geoffrey Chaucer, whose *Canterbury Tales* has become literary canon. The *Confessio Amantis* with its magical lore was equally popular, and surprisingly was neither greatly controversial nor suppressed.

Many more explicitly magical versions of this text exist by a variety of names, including the Book of Enoch and Book of Hermes. The purported origin of the text clearly diverged somewhat over time. Each version includes instructions as to the election of these fifteen talismans and sigils to be engraved upon the corresponding gemstones. Two general variations of sigils have been identified; complex and presumably older versions, and simplified or degenerate forms. The herbs deviate somewhat from the Gower version, and the function of each talisman greatly expanded upon. The textual content is fairly consistent and begins "Quindecim stellis," so this is the name used for convenience among scholars and here.

Cornelius Agrippa includes the simplified sigils and descriptions in his *Three Books of Occult Philosophy* of approximately 1500 AD, along with corresponding pictorial images which do not generally appear in earlier versions of the *Quindecim Stellis* text. Alternate herbs and gemstones are given as well.

The pairing of sigils, gemstones and herbs in the *Quindecim Stellis* lead one to conclude that they are designed primarily for the construction of magical rings, though this is not stated explicitly in the text. This ambiguity permits the creation of loose gemstone talismans either washed in a tea of the herbs listed, or placed in a bag with small amounts of the dried herbs, if needed. My own experience suggests that the ring form of these rings is noticeably more potent, though the loose gemstone talismans are satisfactory.

Agrippa's take on celestial talismans overall favors rings, as he says "When any star ascends fortunately, with the fortunate aspect or conjunction of the Moon, we must take a stone, and herb that is under that star, and make a ring of that metal that is suitable to this star and fasten the stone, putting the herb, or root under it; not omitting the inscriptions of images, names and characters, also the proper suffumigations..."- *Three Books of Occult Philosophy* Bk. I, Chapter 47, (Tyson ed.) page 140.

Some aspects of this deviate from the instructions in the *Quindecim Stellis*, which only permits the Moon applying to conjoin the respective fifteen fixed stars rather than also permitting fortunate aspects. Experimentation by myself and Chris Warnock agrees with the *Quindecim Stellis* over Agrippa.

Because the Moon must apply fairly tightly to a conjunction of a fixed star, if one is on the Ascendant, the other is as well. *Picatrix* strongly disfavors placing the Moon on the Ascendant. "Never put the Moon on the ascendant of anything you wish to do, because she is the ascendant's enemy…" *Picatrix*, Book II, Chapter 3, (Greer-Warnock trans.) My own experience is that talismans made with the Moon on the Ascendant function, but seem to pervert the intention of the user as if they were rebellious servants. Which is the implication of what *Picatrix* here says. I rule out all benevolent talismanic elections which have the Moon on the Ascendant or even the 1st House, and have for several years now.

My original take on the fixed stars has to be revised in a number of instances, since my Ancient Stellar Magic lecture. First, I no longer allow the Moon on the Ascendant; I came to this conclusion shortly after the lectures. Second, the evidence that the Behenian stars can be used as a substitute or a repair for natally afflicted planets of a similar nature is somewhat in doubt. Third, the popularity of the *Quindecim Stellis* is evidence against my notion that this was a toolkit primarily for itinerant magicians; it was simply too widely distributed for that presumably limited audience. Though of great value to itinerant magicians, the ubiquity suggests that this was magic for the masses; at least to the extent of the English-speaking literate classes.

The Lesser Dog Star is given the name Procyon because it rises before Sirius (the Greater Dog Star) on the ecliptic. Romans called it Antecanis, having the same meaning. Some English astronomers called it the Northern Sirius. It is the alpha star of the constellation of the Lesser Dog. It is said to represent Maera, the hound of Icarius who drowned himself from grief at the death of his master.

According to Manilius, the natal influence of Procyon is to endow the native an affinity with hounds of all kinds and skills at making the instruments of hunting, such as nets and spears. However, the natal influence of a fixed star has an unclear relationship with the talismans of the same; sometimes they are completely oppositional in function, unlike planets.

According to Ptolemy, the star is of the nature of Mercury and Mars. This suggests that gold, bronze, silver, and iron are suitable metals for the rings of Procyon. Since the Moon has a prominent place in all fixed star talismanic elections, silver is always acceptable. The fixed stars are said to be the handmaidens of the Sun in *Picatrix*, which suggests gold is viable; this is my experience and preference. Gold is the most temperate of metals, and the Sun has a special role in the divisions of the Tropical ecliptic, so this may suggest that gold is proper for virtually all talismans to an extent. Bronze is an alloy, a mixture of metals; this makes it suitable as a metal for Mercury and things like Mercury. Iron or steel is the metal which has the greatest affinity for Mars, and things which are like Mars.

Though I mean this for the selection of metals in the bands of the rings of Procyon, this is probably applicable for talismans entirely composed of these metals, though I believe the absence of the gemstone will be weaker.

The gemstone listed for Procyon in the *Quindecim Stellis* is agate. Agate is a banded gemstone of chalcedony alternating with quartz. While it comes in an enormous array of colors, there is some indication that the classical form of agate was banded tawny or brown. Because of its banding, it is often associated with Mercury because of his governance over mixed colors and mixtures overall. This is not to suggest that one can substitute agate for another Mercurial stone for a Procyon talisman; this association is very particular.

The herbs given in the *Quindecim Stellis* for Procyon talismans are heliotrope flowers and pennyroyal flowers. Heliotrope is named such because it turns its flowers towards the rays of the Sun, and has very strong Solar associations. Pennyroyal was used in ancient times as a spice and as an abortifacient. It has also been used in various forms as a pesticide. The only obvious thing these two plants have in common is that their delicate flowers are a vivid purple.

When choosing agates for the rings of Procyon, I selected those of a lavender hue; as close as I could get to the color of the flowers.

According to the *Quindecim Stellis,* a Procyon talisman "Grants the favor of God and man, gives men the favor of the spirits of the air, gives great power over magic, and keeps men healthy." The meaning of nearly all but the last prompt some great debates.

Like the talisman of Alphecca from the same text, the Procyon talisman grants the favor of God. It is a very odd notion that a talisman might have any power over a Divine being, at least by modern conceptions of divinity. I have speculated that this might actually mean that it instills moral fiber in the wearer, or an affinity with pious persons and things.

The favor of man obviously suggests popularity, but the favor of spirits of the air is much more confounding. Who are the spirits of the air? In at least one other grimoire this phrase is used as a euphemism for demons; the malevolent fallen angels of the Christian tradition. It is not obvious this is the meaning here, as demons are mentioned elsewhere and the author chooses his words carefully. Angels are not mentioned in the *Quindecim Stellis,* but demons, the spirits of the dead, God, and the spirits of the air are the categories of spiritual beings mentioned. (The Peoples of the Earth are also mentioned, but this probably means human beings rather than the Peoples of the Mound; that is fairies.) My own take is that these are probably nature spirits, at least in this context. Spirits of the air would be invisible naturally, capable of transmitting messages, and raising and dispersing winds.

Giving great power over magic is more ambiguous than it appears. The implication in some translations suggests that this ring bestows a power to resist enchantments, while others suggest that it enhances the magical power of the bearer. Either is quite useful, but to a practicing magician the latter is superior.

It's rare that a talisman can boast an improvement of health overall, but there's one reason why this is particularly plausible with Procyon talismans. Currently the star is at 26 Cancer 01, which means that an applying Moon would by necessity be in the essential dignity known as Rulership or Domicile in any part of Cancer; the strongest essential dignity according to Renaissance sources and ranking a +5 in quantitative dignity tables. The Moon is always a cosignificator or secondary significator in talismanic elections and most elections overall. When a significator is essentially dignified, it improves the health, appearance, social station, and popularity of the subject; or at least greatly increases the chances of that improvement. This also explains the power of the favor of man too.

When multiple significators are essentially dignified, the chances of this wonderful power manifesting with ease greatly increase; this is why we attempt to make the Ascendant and Moon and if possible the Part of Fortune essentially and accidentally dignified and unafflicted to the greatest possible degree, as these are the three primary cosignificators in descending order of importance. We can situate the star or planet on the Median Coeli rather than the Ascendant (as we should in fixed star elections), but I believe the Ascendant must at least be unafflicted and preferably be ruled by a planet which is dignified, unafflicted, and hopefully also not cadent.

Nevertheless, this is speculative to a degree. The position of Procyon in Cancer is temporary; precession is slow but real. Someday Procyon will exit Cancer and the Moon will not be essentially dignified during these elections. How that will impact their function will be for future magicians to discover, as I will surely be long gone by then. It may have great impact or none at all.

Heinrich Cornelius Agrippa gives a somewhat different account of Procyon and its powers. In addition to a sigil somewhat different than the one given in *Quindecim Stellis,* he provides two celestial images for Procyon; a rooster and "three little maids." As the foremost dog star, the rooster may signify a herald as the bird crows at dawn. The double-threefold branching of the sigils may suggest flowers, but the Agrippa version especially seems to derive from a rooster's clawprint. I often think the earlier version resembles the lotus blossom somewhat, but this is not relevant to Procyon by the time of the *Quindecim Stellis* if ever. The association with maidens perhaps suggests the special role of the Moon and her essential dignity in proximity to Procyon, but also strongly echo pictorial representations of the three Graces, Euphrosyne, Aglaia, and Thalia—the personifications of mirth, elegance, and youthful beauty.

The other variant is that Agrippa says Procyon grants power against witchcraft rather than power over magic. In this context, witchcraft is understood to be curses and malevolent fascination. However, this may be a quirk of translation; it is widely known that the J.F. translation from Latin to English is idiosyncratic and at times in clear error. Preference should probably be given to the translations of the older *Quindecim Stellis* texts for the time being. Certainly if Procyon talismans give power over magic, they will resist curses as well to at least some extent.

John Gower gives no description of the function of Procyon, but he says its nature is of Mercury and has a Martial tint. Rather than giving heliotrope and pennyroyal flowers as its herbs, he lists primrose.

Other 3
Event
Sep 15 2017, Fri
9:09 AM EDT +4:00
Holy Name Hospital
Geocentric
Tropical
Alcabitius

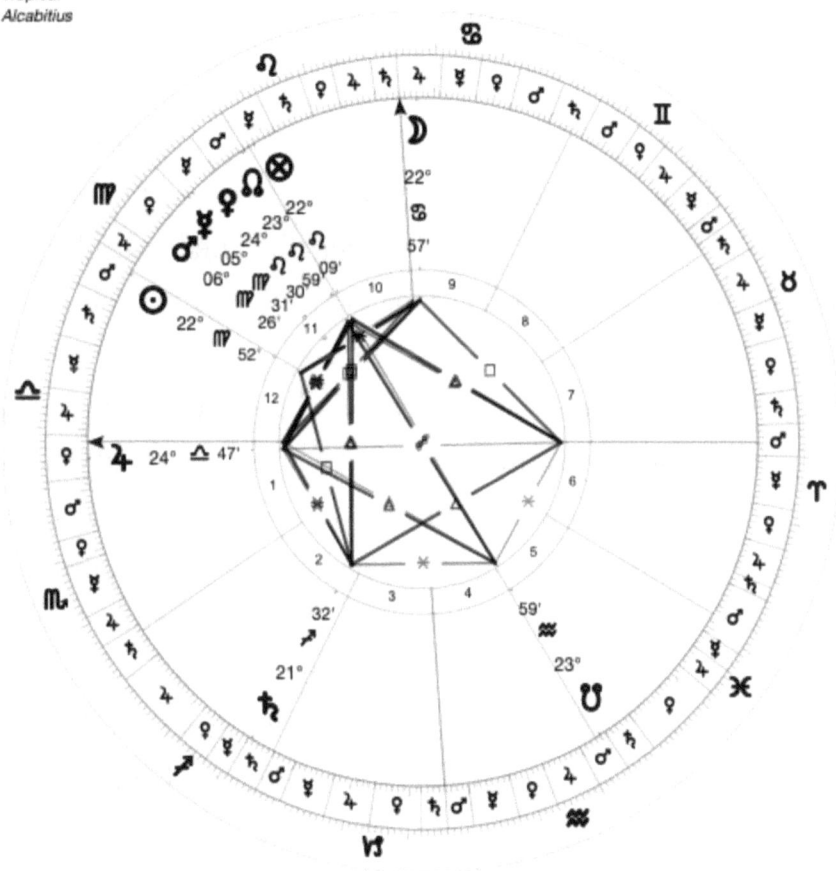

The Moon tightly applies to a conjunction of Procyon. Procyon culminates. The Moon is fast and applying a tight aspect to a Benefic, though this is a square. The Moon is not cadent yet. The Ascendant is greatly fortunated by an applying conjunction with a Fortune; this is Jupiter, which is essentially dignified in Face. The Moon's Sign Ruler is not cadent; it is itself. For the earlier part of the election, the Part of Fortune is applying to conjoin the

North Node, also known as Caput Draconis or Rahu. This greatly strengthens the election by having a tertiary significator conjoined with celestial point similar in nature to a Fortune and generally increases power or benevolence, depending on the canonical source.

Students of Chris Warnock will be perplexed by my usage of the Moon squaring Jupiter in a benevolent election. This is not an error. One of the distinctions between the medieval electional rules of *Picatrix* and the later Renaissance electional rules is that the unchanging nature of the planets takes precedence over the aspects formed between them. So a planet applying to trine Saturn is a fortitude in Renaissance elections but is a great affliction to *Picatrix* because a Malefic is always a Malefic to some extent. Conversely, a planet applying to oppose Venus is an affliction in Renaissance elections but a fortitude in *Picatrix*, because a Fortune is always fortunate. Of course, it is better in benefic elections for significators making trines and sextiles to the Benefics, but even squares and oppositions strengthen the significator better than any aspect to Malefics. In many talismanic elections the configuration will agree with both systems, but not this one. I find *Picatrix* to be more effective with talismanic elections than other sources. Part of why I feel that *Picatrix* is justified with prioritizing the natural qualities of planets over aspects is the angular relationship of the Houses; placing Fortunes on the Ascendant and Midheaven surely must be seen as an exceptionally positive configuration, yet they are in a quartile relationship with one another. *Picatrix* favors Benefics on the Angular cusps, and asserts that Malefics there will ruin elections. Reason suggests that the basic nature of these planets and the strength they lend to these critical points should supersede the aspects between them. It is logical to suppose that the weakness supplied by Malefics on the angles is greater than the strength provided by the Fortunes, because combination of "hard aspects" are similar in nature to the Infortunes and increase their malice.

Nine rings with lavender agate were chosen. Four were made with gold wire wrapped around a gold-filled wire skeleton to enhance durability and structure for myself. Five were made with gold-filled wire for clients.

The suffumigation used was amber resin. Amber is Lunar, and it was selected from a list of alternatives by tarot divination.

No herbs were used because none were available. It happens a lot when working with the Behenian star talismans; the herbs are quite specific and are often hard to obtain. Often these are dangerous herbs, but sometimes they are simply unpopular. Both appeared to be the case with regards to pennyroyal flowers and heliotrope flowers. Neither were available for purchase online. Pennyroyal is probably an abortifacient, but the complete unavailability of heliotrope was unaccountable except a lack of interest. Dried pennyroyal was available, but upon inspection of what was available, did not appear to have any identifiable petals in the mix. Dried heliotrope of any sort was unavailable.

But the election was too excellent to pass up; I decided to make the nine rings and shelve them until I could obtain the dried flowers. That took a long time.

Now, I have to confess something; I have a brown thumb. I'm terrible with plants. It's not that I cause flowers to wilt and blacken by my presence; I just am absent-minded and neglectful of plants, or I overcompensate and drown them. I have graduate-level training in biology, but virtually none in botany. I can't distinguish different types of trees in my neighborhood. Magical plants interest me for certain, but those are usually purchased dry rather than fresh. (Interestingly enough, it hasn't greatly impacted my skill as a rootworker. But many such over the decades have been in urban environments like myself.)

I know that I should remedy this deficit of knowledge and interest, but I also know that I should eat more broccoli too. And I am these days, but you probably can't make me enjoy it.

Enter the generous assistance of Harold Roth, proprietor of alchemy-works.com. He is the opposite of me; he is in love with the magical uses of plants and can grow just about anything. I asked him for help when my attempts to grow heliotrope and pennyroyal in my home produced stunted and listless sprouts which at any moment seemed about to turn brown.

With his help I purchased live plants from a seasonal vendor which did not appear on my online searches, repotted them twice, and set up a medium and eventually large grow tent with a massive grow light and automated waterer presumably designed for marijuana cultivation. To this I added the presence of an SIM talisman I had made years ago as an experiment, which increases the bounty of harvests among other things.

After several months of frustration, labor, a hefty financial investment, and an astronomical electric bill, I finally harvested a handful of heliotrope flowers and several pennyroyal flowers. Just enough to dry and add to the nine rings in a supplementary election which was suitable.

One of the most common questions asked by both beginning and intermediate students of Scholastic Image Magic is what to do when a talisman is incomplete at the end of an electional window. Do you just keep going, is it a failure, or can you finish up at a later time?

It is clear that any significant alteration of a talisman outside of a valid electional window diminishes or destroys its power. My own rule is that the petition, engraving, suffumigations, and addition of herbs must all be completed within the electional window, though I allow polishing, molding the glue and herbs under the rings, and repairing any spillage immediately after the electional window before that sets. The electional window represents the entry of the spirit of time of that hierarchy into the talisman, and as long as the ingredients are fundamentally in place, minor subsequent changes are like the cutting of the umbilical cord after an infant is born, removal of a caul, or even bathing it.

Nevertheless, there are numerous situations where cast talismans are not completed properly, the herbs required cannot be obtained, or other finishing touches are impossible to complete in time. Sometimes one will engrave a cabochon and later wish to set it in a ring or other piece of jewelry. Sometimes a ring or talisman will break and need minor repairs. This is why supplementary elections are necessary.

Chris Warnock's take on supplementary elections (which are quite distinct from attunement elections) are that they should be avoided, but when absolutely necessary the goal is to match the configuration of the secondary election to that of the primary one. No two elections are identical, but for example in a Mercury talismanic election, both should be Mercury Hour and/or Day, and Mercury in as identical a state of essential dignity as can be managed. I would go perhaps a little further and require that Mercury be in the same Sign; to me, there's a qualitative difference between Mercury in Gemini and Mercury in Virgo, and to complete a talisman begun in one in the other will diminish its power.

Either way, it's really hard to do, which is why supplementary elections are best avoided. But there is a loophole, or at least there appears to be one. In one version of the grimoire called the Treasure of Alexander, at the very end of the first planetary ring recipe (for Saturn) it says "If you cannot finish it in the aforementioned configuration wait until the Moon again returns to the aforementioned aspects and signs or is in Cancer." While this is not repeated again in the instructions for the remaining six planets, it suggests a peculiar relationship between Saturn and

Cancer, or something about the Moon in Cancer which allows talismans in general to be completed.

The former is not entirely illogical; Saturn is in Detriment in Cancer, so this is a special relationship. It is, however, a very bad one. The alternative is to conclude that the Moon in Cancer is special somehow.

This is what I believe; since the Moon is cosignificator in most talismanic elections, placing it in rulership specifically allows the talisman to retain power even while being altered so long as the initial election is suitably strong. It is like hooking a surgical patient up to a life support system so that doctors can operate on major organs without killing him or her. My own experiments support this view, as I have performed supplementary elections of this sort several times on talismans which have proven quite powerful afterwards.

In any case, a supplementary election for Procyon often would have to be both kinds of supplementary election; the Moon applying to conjoin Procyon and also be in Cancer. Thus was the case here.

Other 4
Event
Jan 28 2018, Sun
11:15 PM EST +5:00
Holy Name Hospital
Geocentric
Tropical
Alcabitius

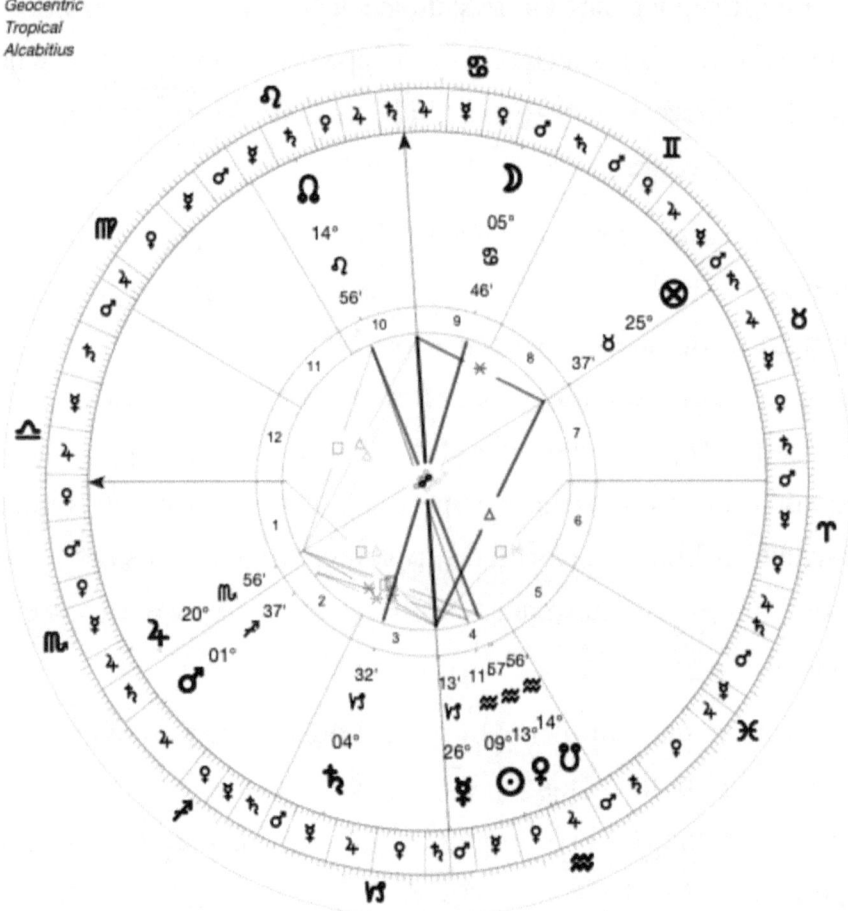

Here we have the Moon applying to conjoin Procyon very loosely on the Midheaven, cadent but extremely fast. The Ascendant Ruler is quite unfortunate; combust and applying to conjoin the South Node. The Moon is unaspected but not void.

Clearly this would be a great cause for concern if this was a normal primary talismanic election, but it is not. Secondary elections only attempt to forge a link with the original celestial hierarchy and to the greatest possible extent any subgroups signified by similar configurations.

While it would be beneficial to have a strong Ascendant Ruler, the primary electional configuration always takes precedence over secondary ones unless the latter is carefully designed to do so. This is actually the logic of using talismans to remedy natal afflictions; these are functionally secondary elections designed to override the planetary influences within the native's astral body, like a splint or an artificial limb. But they have to be elected rather precisely to have that kind of impact. This secondary election does not possess those characteristics. As a Venus talismanic election (which it would have to be), it's a complete flop.

What it does succeed at is placing the Moon in Cancer and having her apply to a conjunction of Sirius on the Midheaven. That's enough to allow a modification of the Procyon talismans without a loss of power.

Once again, I suffumigated with amber and applied the dried flowers and glue under the gemstones. I had some problems with the glue; I used too little and then too much, leading me to have to manage a lot of glue foam overflow and spillage long after the electional window had closed. But the result was clear; the nine Rings of Procyon radiated power and vitality.

Magical rings in the Scholastic Image Magic tradition are one of my great loves, and my favorite text after *Picatrix* is the *Quindecim Stellis*. I began lecturing on this tradition using this grimoire as a platform from which to educate about the wider tradition, but also because I have a particular love and respect for the 8th Sphere, the realm of the fixed stars. The *Quindecim Stellis* is a beguilingly short grimoire, but full of secrets.

I consider the creation of astrological talismans in SIM to be a form of initiation. In a broader sense, the process of education, election, creation, experimentation, and mastery is a more general initiatory ladder, but each planetary hierarchy has its own initiations which one undertakes when creating the talismans and petitions of each respective planet. Yet these are only seven planetary initiatory processes plus the general one; I think there are many more. There are mysteries revealed upon the creation of each of the fifteen Behenian star talismans, each of the thirty-six Faces, and each of the twenty-eight Lunar Mansions. I also think the planets in aggregate have their own initiation, the Faces, the Lunar Mansions, and the Behenian stars when one has worked with them all. My hope is that I may be given the keys to each of these celestial courts within my time here on Earth.

The Home Defense Rings of Al Tarf

Other 6
Event
Feb 21 2013, Thu
9:08 PM EST +5:00
Holy Name Hospital
Geocentric
Tropical
Alcabitius

"The ninth mansion is called Atarf. It begins in at 12 degrees 51 minutes and 26 seconds of Cancer and ends at 25 degrees 42 minutes and 51 seconds of the same sign. In this Mansion it is good... to help a man defend himself from being attacked by another man."

Not the most obvious election; Al Tarf is primarily used for curses, but this was the last benevolent election for this Mansion for some time to come, and took the opportunity.

My hope is that the Moon's trine with a virtually stationary Mercury in extreme essential debility will cause potential attackers to stumble and freeze.

The Ring of the Casino

Other 7
Event
Jul 23 2014, Wed
5:49 AM EDT +4:00
Holy Name Hospital
Geocentric
Tropical
Alcabitius

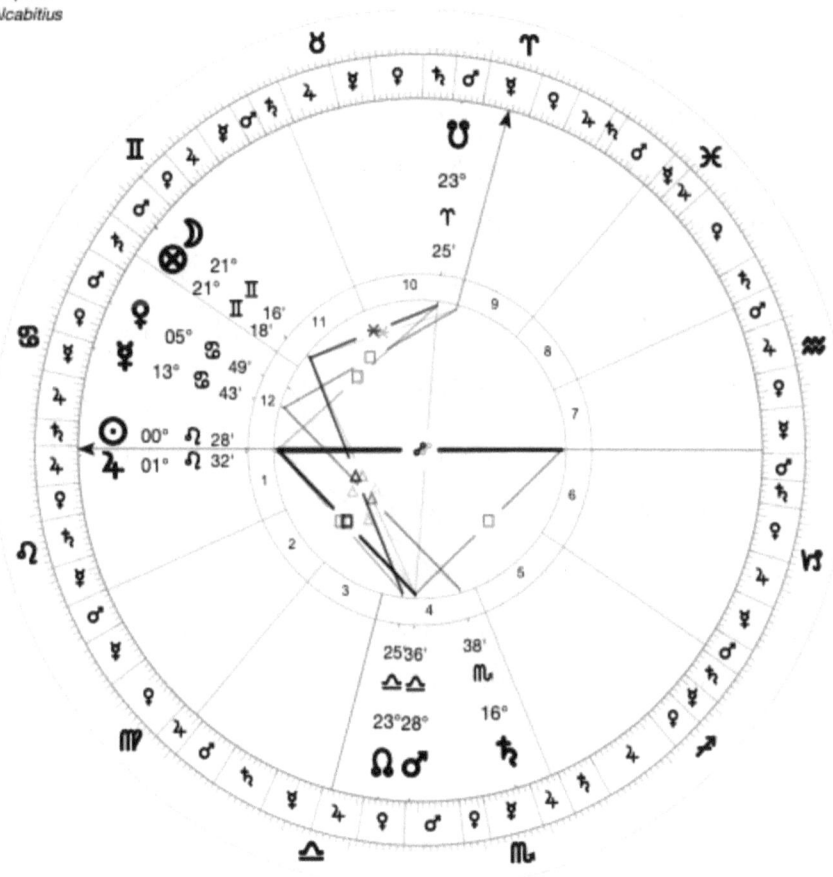

Picatrix: "There rises in the second face of Cancer a woman with a beautiful face, and on her head she has a crown of green myrtle, and in her hand is a stem of the plant called water lily, and she is singing songs of love and joy. This is a face of games, wealth, joy and abundance. This is its form."

In other sources it adds that it bestows the love of women, which is probably a side effect of the affinity the talismanic image creates in people, places, and things depicted therein.

The Moon trining Mars is an affliction, but as the Moon is waning it's not all that bad. The Day/Hour of Mercury definitely adds to the electional power. The Moon's Sign ruler being cadent would normally rule out this election, but having a benefic on the ASC offsets this. Unfortunately, Jupiter is combust but I still think it's enough to offset this effect. The Sun is greatly strengthened, however, by conjoining Jupiter and in elections which prioritize the Sun (as most Face elections do) the role of the Moon is lessened as she is always subservient to the Sun.

So, it's not the best election but I think it'll work. It's an upgrade from my former Somachalmais rings.

Four agates in gold were used; three yellow and one brown agate. Attraction Oil was used in this instance, and the suffumigation and herb beneath the stones were gum arabic.

The Ring of Fever's Eclipse

Other 8
Event
Apr 15 2014, Tue
12:50 AM EDT +4:00
Holy Name Hospital
Geocentric
Tropical
Alcabitius

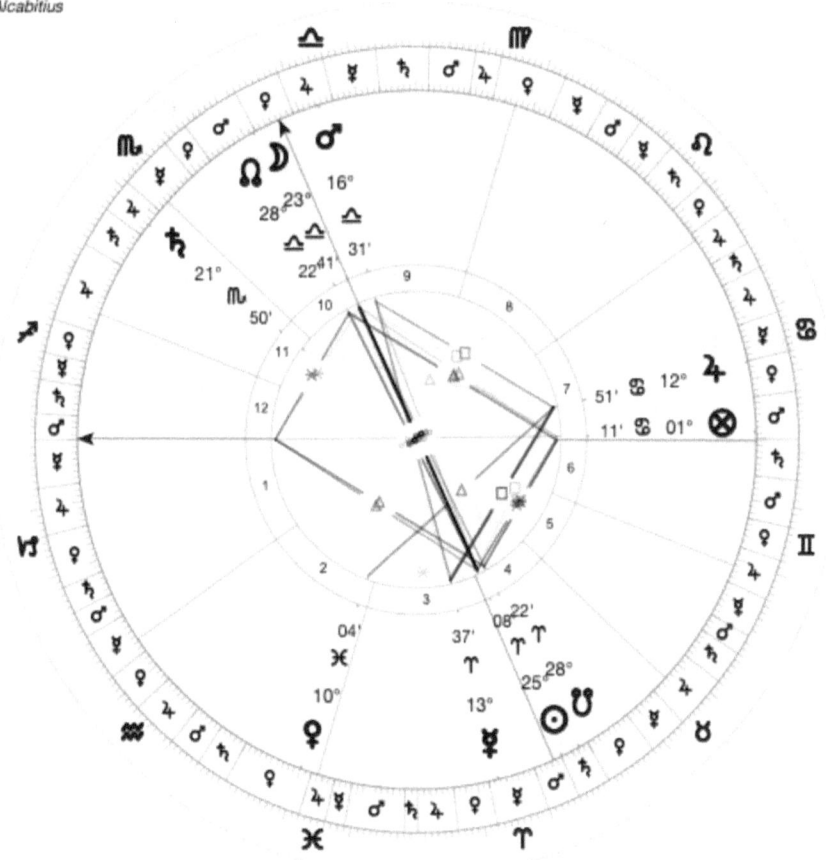

This one is one of the riskier elections I've done recently, to the point it almost falls out of Tradition. It's a talismanic election for Arcturus, but the Moon is tightly applying to a Lunar eclipse.

Traditional sources disagree whether a Full Moon is benefic or malefic, but the Traditional contemporary consensus is that elections are to be avoided involving eclipses. The loophole, if there is one, is that in *mundane* eclipses whose angles are ruled by the benefics and/or the Sign of the principal Luminary, presage a period of peace, prosperity, and health for the kingdom.

Sources are silent on whether this can be extended to elections, but my need for an Arcturus talisman was strong and consultation with tarot repeatedly indicated that these talismans would be benevolent and potent.

The Moon was tightly applying to Arcturus on the MC as well as the benevolent North Node. The Asc and MC were ruled by the benefics, both in their exaltations. This was immediately before the beginning of the proper Lunar Eclipse, which was cadent in the 9th.

"Plantain juice with seeds or rooted placed under jasper, especially green [jasper], carries away fevers and restrains the flow of blood."

Green jasper was used with the name Arcturus above the *Quindecim Stellis* sigil. Crumbled plantain chips and two types of plantain seeds were glued beneath the stones. Luckymojo Healing Oil was used, and the suffumigation was lignum aloes and plantain chips. Four rings were created and four loose gemstones/pendants.

As an experiment, I toyed with planetary dieting as a preparation for the working by eating most of the plantain chips so that I was digesting it during the talismanic election.

I'll either have eight really strong healing talismans or eight really strong plague talismans. No one said this stuff was without danger.

(Postscript: These turned out to be incredibly dangerous talismans, and were eventually thrown into the ocean.)

The Ring of Splendor

The talisman of Zachor, the 2nd Face of Leo

Other 9
Event
Sep 11 2014, Thu
6:38 AM EDT +4:00
Holy Name Hospital
Geocentric
Tropical
Alcabitius

This was a highly experimental talisman. It not only used a somewhat imperfect election, but the decan's attributes are largely unpleasant. And yet, I believe it is actually rather desirable in extreme.

"There rises in the second face of Leo a man who wears a crown of white myrtle on his head, and he has a bow in his hand. This is a face of beauty, riding, and the ascension of a man who is ignorant and base, and this is a face of war and naked swords. This is its form."

By ensuring the principal planets (here Jupiter, Sun, and Moon) are unafflicted and accidentally dignified by aspects with other planets, the negative attributes of the Face are suppressed and the positive ones (beauty, riding, and perhaps promotion) brought forth.

Nevertheless, Jupiter squares Saturn and other planets aspect the malefics. So how is this resolved? By putting both malefics in the 3rd House, whose cadency restrains their mischief. Furthermore, the Moon is also cadent, but in any election which depends on the Sun, the Moon's state is less important. The main strength of the election beyond meeting the minimal conditions required, is that the Sun is applying to a conjunction of the Lesser Benefic. Venus is dignified and debilitated, but more of the former; if the end result of this is that the beautification endowed is somewhat of a sexier nature, I won't be complaining.

I also wish to point out that Face talismans have an odd tendency to fascinate and win over people who resemble the image in some way. It's probably not a bad thing to have power over powerful, ignorant and vile people, particularly if there is war and unsheathed swords nearby. This actually may be the greater value of this type of talisman.

My preferred stone-beryl- was unavailable, but pyrite was substituted and set in gold and gold-filled wire. The suffumigation was balsam and basil-the former from

Harold Roth; without whose help this project would have been impossible. The same mixture was combined with Gorilla Glue and put under the cabochons. Seven rings were made for myself, though the last took long and my hand became fatigued and unsteady so it may be less potent than the others. The rings were anointed with Luckymojo.com's Attraction Oil at various phases of the operation.

The image was used, depicting a naked male figure with a crown of flowers (or flowers in his hair) holding a bow, sometimes with an arrow as well. The sigil of Zachor was put on the chest along with that of Jupiter (conventional sigil) and the word BEAUTY inscribed above the figure and ZACHOR below.

I am not sure how this talisman works. It may help with physical fitness, prove itself the medieval botox and lap band, or simply create a glamour. I am also not completely certain that the "war and unsheathed swords" part is fully suppressed, but I am hopeful.

The Talismans of Turmantis

The Talismans of the Second Decan of Scorpio

Other 10
Event
Nov 10 2017, Fri
6:17 AM EST +5:00
Holy Name Hospital
Geocentric
Tropical
Alcabitius

The Sun rises in the Second Face of Scorpio in the Hour of the Sun, the Moon is fast and applying to a square of the Sun and then the North Node of the Moon. The North Node is conjunct the Midheaven. The Moon is waning, but this is suitable for the purpose of the talismans. The Descendant is weak, potentially giving more relative power to the Sun on the Ascendant. Since putting fortunes or any dignified planets on the Ascendant and Midheaven require a quartile aspect, I consider this configuration beneficent; this is especially so with the aspects of the quarters of the Moon, with the exception of the combustion of the Moon. The Sun himself applies to a wide conjunction with a benefic, strengthening him a tiny bit. The Moon is applying an aspect to the Ruler of the Sign she is in; this would be better if it were a sextile or trine, but it does add power. It's a good, solid configuration, if not absolutely perfect. For those of you who need a refresher, this is what *Picatrix* has to say about Faces, also known as Decans:

"Note that each of the twelve signs is divided into three equal parts, and these divisions are called faces. Each of these faces has its own images, forms and figures, as the sages of India have recounted, and to each of the faces is assigned one of the seven planets. These faces are divided and distributed according to the position and order of the planets, beginning at the highest and proceeding in order all the way to the lowest, and then returning to the highest as we will explain. Beginning with Aries, the first face is assigned to Mars, the second to the Sun which follows him in order, the third to Venus who follows the Sun, and the first face of Taurus to Mercury; it proceeds in this way through the order of the planets until the end of the signs. Each of these faces has a nature and image that is appropriate to its lord; and we will present each of the images that arise in each of the faces in the following pages." -*Picatrix* II:11

At the end of the section, *Picatrix* details the somewhat unique requirements for the election of a Face talisman:

"When you make any of images of the faces described above, make them in a material appropriate to the planet that rules the face; then the work will be as we have said- that is, if you make the image when the corresponding planet is present in that face, then that work will be perfect and it will manifest in the world. If it happens that the Sun is rising in the hour of the planet or combines its force with it in a way that you desire, the work will be stable and strong. In what we have said above, beware that the quality of the planet be not overcome by the Sun. If, on the other hand, you understand the reasons for everything that has already been said, the images of the faces we have given will bring about the effects you wish powerfully and completely." -*Picatrix* II:11

I have a particular love for Face talismans. I think the greatest secrets of Scholastic Image Magic are hidden within them, and have lectured about some of what I have discovered elsewhere. Although the Second Face of Scorpio is not one which most would leap at; I think it has hidden excellences and is worth another look.

"There rises in the second face of Scorpio a man riding a camel, holding a scorpion in his hand. This is a face of knowledge, modesty, settlement, and of speaking evil of one another. This is its form." - *Picatrix* II:11

The images of the Faces are constructed by the planetary rulerships of the Signs, sometimes proximal Decans, and the activating planet. The scorpion in the image iconography represents the Sign of Scorpio. Camels in general are ruled by the Sun, and so the camel here is the representation of the Sun in the middle of Scorpio. The man may represent the user or may represent Mars, the ruler of Scorpio; this is why in my design I gave him a pointed helmet. The properties of the Face talisman rarely relate directly to the image, but instead the interactions of the properties of the activating planet, the Sign ruler, and even the triplicity of the Sign in parallel with the pictorial symbols. So is the case here.

The name Turmantis comes from the *Liber Hermetis* of the 1st Century. That text largely ascribes each of the 36 Faces to regions of the known world at the time and a series of images whose purpose is not described, though one may assume they are for the purpose of gaining benefits in each region. They are one of the few sources which give names to the Faces, and function as the name of the Face's lord. The spirits of the Faces like it, and it's more memorable and usually shorter than saying or inscribing or writing X Face of Y.

So, what does it do? Scorpio is probably the least pleasant of all the Decanic triads. The 1st Face is about suffering and anger, and the 3rd is for rape (and should never be used.) The 2nd Face is a mix of good and bad, but there's definitely bad. Or at least dark.

- Knowledge
- Modesty
- Settlement
- Speaking evil against another

I chose this election largely because of the first attribute; knowledge. Scorpio often is associated with secrets and the presence of the Greater Luminary, the Sun is the revelation of hidden knowledge.

However, I admit that the fourth attribute is also intriguing. In this era of outrage and memetic warfare, an enhanced capacity for imprecation might not be unhelpful. Or maybe I'll get some juicy gossip. Here the sting of the scorpion is set ablaze by the fire of the Sun, and a victim's fame is poisoned into infamy.

Modesty is something we all could benefit from a little. I'm not yet sure why it is an attribute of this Face.

Settlement perhaps suggests peacemaking, or perhaps settling for less? Setting down roots? I'm not sure what that means in this context; *Picatrix* can sometimes be elusive in this context. It also appears in the attributes of the 1st Face of Scorpio, so perhaps this has more to do with the nature of Scorpio than the particular interaction with the Sun.

Nevertheless, when a Face talisman's electional configuration is benevolent those qualities will predominate, and when it is malevolent the latter will.

Two talismans were created using large and medium bloodstone cabochons. I placed one on my Sun altar and the other in a black flannel mojo-style bag along with the Solar herbs cinnamon, calamus, and lemongrass. The colors of Turmantis are black, yellow and tan; so I chose a black bag. I wore gold and black during the election; the former representing the Sun and something approximating the yellow for the Face's second color. The suffumigation was frankincense resin.

At the top is the name of the Face, Turmantis. At the bottom is the power I most desired, knowledge. It is fairly standard practice to inscribe the purpose of a talisman in this manner as noted in *Picatrix* if there is space, especially if some of the other powers are less desirable. In the center is a helmeted warrior riding a bactrian camel; he holds a scorpion in his right hand. On the back of the gemstone is an X, normally this is used when the image of a celestial hierarchy is unknown, but my goal was to use this to overcome any defects of design. There almost was one.

The sigil I intended to inscribe which appears in purple was intented to be the sigil of Turmantis, which is exactly like what I engraved except it has a third circle at the apex. The sigils of the Faces we derive from charakteres on a Syrian defixio from the 5th or 6th century. Instead, I inscribed the Latin *Picatrix* sigil of the Sun, which is very similar and easy to confuse at 6 am sans coffee. This might have been a problem in a different configuration, but fortunately placing the sigil of a Face activator on the talisman of a Face is quite appropriate, and even deemed mandatory by Renaissance writers such as Cornelius Agrippa. Close call, but still good. I'm glad I made these for myself.

The Rings of the Diplomat

Sirius culminating, with a tightly applying conjunction of the Moon; the very fast Moon applying to both Benefics, and the Greater Benefic on the Ascendant

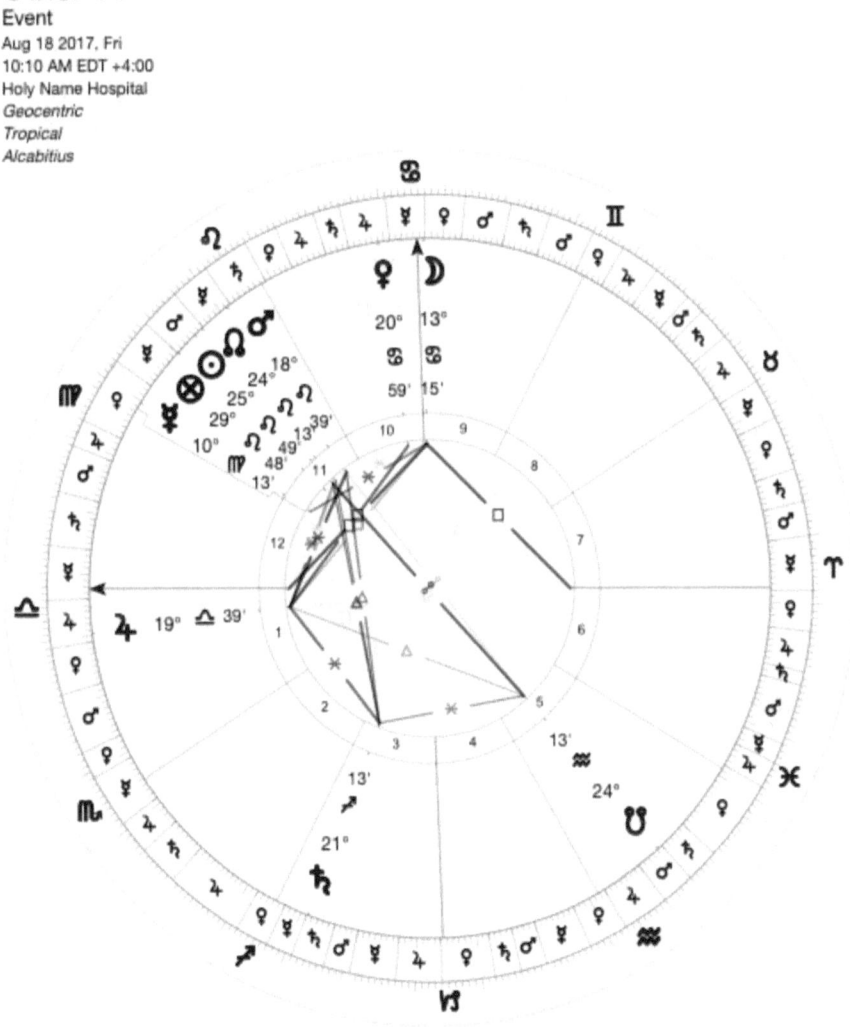

While Jupiter is somewhat afflicted, overall this is a superb election for Sirius. The speed of the Moon, the Benefic on the

Ascendant, and the amazing tightness of the conjunction of the Moon with Sirius on the Midheaven were all great fortitudes that together provided an election that is quite powerful and proportionately rare.

For the time being I don't believe the solar eclipse of August 21 will have had a significant impact upon these elections; they ought to be fully out of orb.

This is an election that I've been eager to try out for an exceptionally long time.

Under the Greater Dog Star, they made an image of a hound and a little virgin; it bestoweth honour and good will, and the favor of men, and aerial spirits, and giveth the power to pacify and reconcile kings, princes, and other men. –Cornelius Agrippa

And elsewhere:

One part savine juniper juice with wormwood and bistort and a little serpent's tongue put under a golden beryl, etc., grants the favor of the spirits of the air and the peoples of the earth, and brings peace and concord between kings and other potentates, and between husbands and wives. –Qundecim Stellis

The oldest obtainable coverage is more general and possibly is confused with the listing for Procyon which follows it in the text, and has no listed powers:

And Canis Major in his like

The fifte sterre is of magique,

The whos kinde is Venerien,

As seith this astronomien.

His propre ston is seid berille,

Bot for to worche and to fulfille

Thing which to this science falleth,

Ther is an herbe which men calleth

Saveine, and that behoveth nede

To him that wole his pourpos spede.

–The *Confessio Amantis* of John Gower

All things being equal, I lean towards the *Quindecim Stellis* as canonical over Agrippa's fixed star sections; particularly the sigils. The *Confessio Amantis* material is valuable too, but mostly to reduce ambiguities and illustrate the evolution of the text.

To clarify this, talismans of Sirius:

- Make people like and obey the wearer.
- Make spirits like and obey the wearer.
- Allows the wearer to resolve disputes between lovers.
- Allows the wearer to resolve disputes between people of leadership and renown.

I've long said that the Ring of the Pleiades is the most important in the *Quindecim Stellis*; the most fundamental in plying one's trade as an itinerant magician in the Early Modern Period. The Rings of either the Greater or Lesser Dog Stars and the Ring of Alkaid would be the ones to follow it; but considering that Sirius is the brightest star of all, it probably takes the lead. A magician with a Sirius ring would be able to be a supreme counselor for his liege or patron, and assist him or her in the governance of their fiefdom or estate. In exchange for generous payment.

On a personal level, I'm close to finally completing the full set of fifteen Behenian talismans as described in the *Quindecim Stellis*. Though a few of these I no longer have in my possession, the process of creating thirteen of these over the past decade have been as powerful an initiation as anything I can imagine. It hasn't been easy, and when the fifteenth is completed I'm going to enjoy a nice bottle of champagne to celebrate.

Four rings were ensouled. The gemstones were golden beryl (with heavy inclusions) in silver bands. I would have prepared more, but golden beryl is very hard to obtain right now. I was indecisive about the suffumigation, and tarot suggested pine resin—not an obvious choice, but there's little canonical guidance on this matter.

Obtaining the wormwood was easy. Obtaining the savine juniper was slightly more challenging. Bistort was difficult, and the chunks were hard to secure under the ring.

But serpent's tongue is not for the squeamish. I ordered preserved constrictors from an educational supply house and dissected half. The process of rooting for the tongue was disgusting, and finding it inside a dead snake challenging. I have done some graduate-level work in Biology, and I don't envy anybody with less training doing something like this. Just nasty.

The serpent's tongue, just to be clear, is not a euphemism for an herb. It's an organ cut from the body of a dead snake. There are no substitutions on this one. And it's arguably the most important of the ingredients after the beryl itself, because of the associations between the persuasiveness and deceptiveness of a serpent, and its mythical speech.

I haven't seen any effects from the one I'm currently wearing, but it clearly emanates power. I can hardly wait to see what this one will do.

The Talismans of the Angel with the Backwards Head
Strong Capella election with the ASC Ruler Retrograde

Other 12
Event
Oct 3 2015, Sat
5:34 AM EDT +4:00
Holy Name Hospital
Geocentric
Tropical
Alcabitius

This article is no longer useful for the purpose it was written, but I retain it here as an educational example.

So, I never post talismanic elections in the future that I intend to use because I find that ruins them. I won't be using this one.

"Horehound seed mixed with equal parts of mint, wormwood and mandrake, placed etc., exalts men to honors, and brings them the favor of kings and nobles, and heals toothache, and is very medicinal."

The stone is sapphire, which can be obtained fairly inexpensively if you search for star sapphire rather than the typical cut and grade of sapphire. Make sure the stone is black or blue; some modern corundums in other colors are sold under the name sapphire but are not such by the older nomenclatures.

The Moon applies very tightly to Capella on the MC. The Moon is triumphed by separating from Jupiter (not visible in the chart) and applying to Venus. The Moon is fast, and in a benevolent Mansion. The Ruler of the Moon's Sign is Angular.

The ASC Ruler is relatively fast, Dignified, and applying to the North Node. It is also applying to a sextile of Saturn, but Mercury and Saturn get along quite well (and the Moon is waning) so I consider this a modest weakness.

Here's the problem: The ASC Ruler is Retrograde.

Some of us believe that in fixed star elections the role of the ASC Ruler is irrelevant. I don't.

Nevertheless, this is a science and we must experiment. Perhaps this can be further clarified.

I invite you to put it to the test. If your talisman provides what you seek within one year, I may well have been proven wrong. But please note any side effects or frustrations resulting from the afflicted Ascendant. After all...

"Never place a retrograde planet as the lord of the ascendant or the lord of the petition because, if either one is retrograde, the petition will be delayed and put at a distance and will not go forward; this is what a retrograde reveals and demonstrates." *Picatrix Rubeus*, page 73.

www.ingramcontent.com/pod-product-compliance
Lightning Source LLC
Chambersburg PA
CBHW032150160426
43197CB00008B/846